The Eye of the Moon

by Shelley Davidow

The Habit of Rainy Nights Press
Portland, Oregon

1st Printing, July, 2007

The Eye of the Moon
ISBN: 978-0-9746683-2-1

Cover Photo by Åsa Tordenmalm
Book & Cover design by Duane Poncy

Published by
The Habit of Rainy Nights Press
Portland, Oregon
http://rainynightspress.org

*B*ranches litter the riverbanks from the summer flood some months before, and the sun is bright in a harsh and merciless sky. This is where we meet. Secretly. I wait for him behind the tree, and he drives up in a gold Toyota automatic. It's the car they share.

The Toyota is dusty from the wheels up. The gold doors are splashed with hardened mud. Winter, in this part of South Africa, is brief and dry. The veld turns to gold and night after night, fires light up the horizons, fires that turn the ground to black, and the air to gray. In the mornings, skeletons of small animals lie scattered across the burnt earth, and the smell of ash and decay is bitter in the wind.

His body trembles through the rough knit of a wool jersey she made.

He thinks the age difference bothers me. He imagines that I lie awake at night and wish that he were ten, no, twenty years younger. He can't penetrate the thoughts or the imagination, which for years has been constructing this in its erotic intensity.

I don't care about age at this point. I'm so wrapped up in the terror and lust that accompany these meetings that I keep telling him to be quiet, that he should not mention the word Time, since it is an illusion.

The water that is so dark and murky carries Bilharzia. When I was younger, I was ill for months until it was discovered that the culprit was a tropical disease that lived in the snail shells in the depth of such stagnant waters as these. In the long summers, my half-brothers and I swung over the river that ran past our house, hanging onto the tender willow reeds until they broke and we fell into the water.

This is not the first time that we've met on the riverbank. It's been going on since summer. No one is aware of this, though I think she knows. My family, who live further along this same road on the river, are utterly unaware that I am now secretive, insincere. They don't sense that most of my words now are only half-truths, since everything relates to him, to The Journalist, whom they know as someone else.

I'm too old and too young for seventeen. I've seen too much of certain things - blood and death and poverty.

My mind weaves a passionate erotic tapestry. But my lips tremble on his and I won't open my mouth even though my body aches with the heat of the African desert.

He was a journalist years ago, before I was born. I met him first when I was twelve. He tells me now that he's loved me since then. He wanted to keep his thoughts pure, and now it's almost too late. If I would just hold him at arm's length, he says, we could avert this imminent catastrophe- avert this horrible betrayal of ideals. All it would take would be for me to wake in the morning, and find that some Angel of Common Sense has breathed upon me, and I no longer feel anything for him. He says this and we smile, but from the advantageous and almost arrogant future, you could look back and see that his smile is already broken around the edges.

She has a name, but I can't say it anymore. I've known her as long as I've known him. She's older than he is. I can never look at her properly again. She will never acknowledge me as an individual, it's not possible. I see myself through her eyes all the time and project myself years into the future, watch the pattern repeat itself, only this time I am the one who is betrayed. I am convinced of this even then, know it somehow with a hollow certainty. At seventeen I am selfish, taking him, this forty-six-year-old, for myself.

In Africa the clichés that existed seemed different from those that played themselves out in the rest of the world. I was unconscious of clichés. It was only later, when The Journalist was in the past, that I read Middlemarch, Lolita, and a hundred others, and found my secret reiterated in numerous versions. It was then that I became aware of something far larger than my individual life, some truth that played itself out again, and again, mercilessly through the ages.

I live with the knowledge that this story will quite certainly be told again.

In the years before The Journalist, you could wake to the song of birds and the rustling of grass. You learned the formidable ways of the wilds as you learned geography at school: snakes; scorpions; lions; mesas; buttes; the Great Rift Valley; how to put out a bushfire or suck poison out of a snake bite. Every morning there passed through your heart an indescribable joy. You loved to be alive, to be you, to be where you were in Africa. You never wanted to leave. You swore to your friends who had already planned escaping the violent, decaying outpost of white colonialism, that you were here, you would stay.

And then one day, you left. For America. This was after The Journalist. There was no way of making money. You had fallen in love with someone else.

You thought America was where people went who wanted to become writers.

Before I knew The Journalist, I was someone who sat on a swing and climbed the tree over the rusted yellow veld. I was the girl, who on her ninth birthday, felt sad because the stoned photographer who happened to drop in that day, took photographs of everyone but her. She thought that because of this incident, her presence on her birthday would be erased from memory. In the future, she thought of that specific day as happening without her. But the day itself is clear, also the tree, with the dove's nest and two small eggs, and the slanting tree-house carpeted with left-over carpet tiles - a spot you could not rest on for long because of the precarious slant of the branches.

There was the mother who gave birth at home, a month overdue, sick with Toxemia. I heard them say, crazy woman.

In the adjoining room, which had a fire burning in the fireplace because it was midwinter in Africa, a girl of eleven heard her mother crying and said, why, why is she crying - and they wouldn't answer her intelligently or directly and she hated them for it, for not understanding that she already knew anyway, but wanted them to speak to her. Hated them for not seeing that the inside of an eleven-year-old's universe is larger than out. At last they spoke grudgingly and admitted that when the baby comes out, it's sometimes painful - but she cried for far too long. The mother. Then the girl heard the baby's cry, and rushed into the room, saw blood, so much - as if someone had been killed - saw the blue cord and the tiny dry wrinkled body that was purple, and the nails that had grown so long in the womb, they had to be cut immediately. The ambulances arrived because the mother was hemorrhaging.

The girl said, my mother nearly died, on the phone to the grandmother - she felt proud that the mother had not died, had made it despite all saying crazy woman - so she said with pride, my mother nearly died.

We did not make love for an entire year. The thoughts and the dreams and the touching were more inescapable than any act of penetration. For a year I learned slowly, the shape of his hands, the way the hairs caught between the slats of his watchstrap. I breathed in the smell of the skin that was so much older than mine, touched the hair already gray at the temples. With closed eyes I traced the line from forehead to chin, the place where his ears joined his face and where the skin, worn and tired from forty-six years beneath the harsh sun, folded up in wrinkles. When he smiled, his face folded up in wrinkles. But from a distance, he had the face of a boy.

I've thought of my life as a narrative ever since I can remember. Each event framed itself, and at the moment of its framing, I caught it forever in my image cavern. I went back into the cavern often, as if to remind myself of what I dared not lose.

There's no distinction between the dream-space in writing and the dream-space in love; they exist for themselves. That was why it happened with The Journalist through writing.

In the back seat of the car, gold on the outside, I wriggle away from him and open the window. It's grown dark and the stars are huge. Several of Jupiter's moons are visible lately even through the lens of a pair of binoculars.

"One day it'll happen to me," I tell him.

"What?"

"I'll be there, just like an extra limb, yours maybe, and you'll find some other woman, someone younger, with darker hair, more youth."

"Don't be ridiculous."

The crickets are loud in the grass at the side of the car. He wants to make love and I refuse. He says he understands, but I know that he doesn't. I think then, about patterns in the universe, how every action has a consequence. I'm not quite sure yet how it works, but I'm beginning to feel as though my life has taken on a form where there are recurrent recognizable threads. This is how I know that one day the situation will reverse itself, and I will find myself on the other side of the looking glass, older, jilted, divested of myself.

"It will happen to me exactly as it's happening to her. I'm absolutely sure."

There is a party at the end of the year, and it is filled with friends. In the newspapers, one reads of unrest and on the streets on Sunday mornings, one steps briefly over blood trails. All these images swirl around the garden at the party. I have a few friends who have come from the townships for the party. They catch mini-bus taxis, despite the daily taxi wars. If my friends aren't lucky, a territorial taxi lord who wants to claim a certain route as his own might take it upon himself to murder any offending taxi-driver and all his passengers. My friends risk their lives just to move in and out of their places, but they smile anyway and laugh and joke with all of us, eating heartily. Live for the day, they say. What choice is there anyway? Sometimes someone with a car will offer to take the township friends home, but this too, is a risk. If the driver of the car is white, and the group runs into any militant Pan-Africanists, they might be killed. The townships at night are desolate, silent, smoky. Pot holes line the roads and fires smolder in rusty drums. Sewerage runs anywhere downhill. Courtesy of Apartheid, we say. People hide inside, afraid of the police, afraid of being branded informers by their own people and necklaced with burning tires. But there is the belief that this will end. Eventually. The Journalist is at the party because he is invited. No one seems to think it strange that I am with him. It's chilly and I walk to the bottom of the garden. This is the last time that I will be there, together with all of my closest friends, in an Africa at the brink of transformation, but I don't know this, and so don't appreciate their presence. I only think about The Journalist, and the night, and when he will leave and go back to her. I attribute my nervous, painful euphoria to The Journalist. He has told one other journalist friend about me. I'm unaware of the way in which the journalist friend will be significant.

Later, looking back on this night, I understand the point of no return, where I unlocked myself from my own reality and began to slide into The Journalist, that world.

In the white light of the moon I held his naked body to me. He smelled strange, smelled too old. I didn't think that. Or if I did, I committed the thought to silence. I didn't want to be on the back seat of a car. It was Friday, and the African Pentecostal church had begun its hymns. The voices floated through the air, as strong and rich as the earth in summer. The voices would not be shut out. I should be elsewhere, I thought. Not in Africa.

It was painful, and I was delirious, unprepared. I pushed him away and then kissed him. I loved him more than I cared about anything else. Voices grew louder through the grass. The singing had stopped and soon in the moonlight, the flowing robes of the church-goers appeared. The Journalist pulled me down under his body, covered me with his body. The crosses that hung from their necks caught white light. They looked in surprise at the gold Toyota parked in the grass so late at night. They must have feared it at first, and then taken note of the white naked body over mine, and hid their faces in shame. Their voices quietened. I didn't understand the language but the focus of it. Shame, I thought I understood them saying. Shame on you, shame.

$$\mathcal{2}$$

Cape Town. One year later. We behave like a couple, do all the things that couples do. He writes poetry to me and we walk on the dazzling beaches and dig crystals from the mountains, but I am uneasy. The beauty of the mountains is unbearable. It presses down on me.

"You are the only lover I ever want to have," he says. And it's always painful, always like the first time. I start to think that there is something wrong with me. The pleasure never blots out the pain. Sometimes it's so severe that he has to stop. He broods, paces the wooden floor of the house and rubs his unshaven chin.

I always look at the way the blue cotton of his shirt catches the hairs on his wrist as he moves his hands. I say that I want to get out of Africa and he smiles.

"It's just a phase you're going through," he says.

At this stage I haven't published anything, but I want to be a writer. I write all the time, late into the night, anywhere, on the floor, the beach. I want to study, but don't have the money.

Sometimes he goes to see her. When she is in a bad way. Because he has broken her heart, he feels responsible, wants to still be her friend, so to say. I grow very uncomfortable about these visits. I don't know when they happen. He tells me afterwards. He says, "I keep telling her, she's doing much better than she thinks. But it breaks my heart, she looks terrible."

"Stop telling me how she is. I can't stand it. Don't ever say anything about her to me again."

I begin to wish that he did not have so many wrinkles on his face. I can see that everyone assumes I am his daughter by the way they respond to us when we go out to eat, if we can afford to.

⚘

The issue is always money. I don't have any. I can't find a job even waitressing because the waiting list for such positions is endless. And the people who work in restaurants have degrees, in Science or Drama or Botany. There are no jobs for them in their fields.

After I return from Cape Town my family takes out a loan against their house, and I go to university. I work hard and realize that the Muse who inspired Keats, Wordsworth, Shelley is redundant. I cannot get beyond a C, because I will not look on Caliban as the Colonized and Prospero as the archetypal Colonizer in Shakespeare Against Apartheid. Instead Apartheid is in itself according to me an enactment of some bitter archetype.

⚘

In retrospect I detect in myself an almost arrogant unwillingness to take part in the university era of my life. As though I somehow thought myself beyond it.

I am a consistent and satisfactory C student.

Then I meet The African Literature Guy, a lecturer who speaks softly and swallows his words so that I have to strain to hear what he's saying. He is originally Zimbabwean, but left Zimbabwe for South Africa after the War for Independence.

"I was a medic," he says. "I didn't want to be a soldier. I didn't believe in the war for a minute. I was sent to the frontline anyway. When I tried to escape to go to university after eighteen months, I was stopped, sent back into the bush for the most violent part of the war." He doesn't say much more about the war. He doesn't even dream about it, he says. We are sitting inside the university on the concourse, a cold hard tiled interior that looks like a giant cafeteria sparsely furnished with plastic tables and chairs.

When I look at his legs beneath his jeans and his hand flat on the floor I think to myself, it could be that I will sleep with him.

I hide that thought horribly under the blanket at night, as I lie next to The Journalist.

The African Literature Guy gives me a short story he has written and I give him a book. We take each other's words home, and when we meet the following day, neither one of us knows what to say. The book and the short story both begin in the afternoon in the Highveld. A man is walking down a dirt road, hitch-hiking. The sun is high in the deep, African sky, and a farmer in a pick-up stops his truck in the dust to give the man a ride. My man is dark-skinned, and his man is light-skinned. From there onwards, the stories change, but our story begins to take shape. Each day it is evident that this event of synchronicity of stories may never happen to either one of us again.

It was The African Literature Guy who introduced me to an editor at a small press. I had the manuscript of the dark man hitchhiking in the sun. One day The African Literature Guy arrived at my doorstep in jeans and a yellow T-shirt. I opened the door to sunlight. He sat with me on the floor. The Journalist sat on the couch. The African Literature Guy said: "the old man, the editor, was sick on Tuesday and so took home your manuscript to read since it was sitting on the top of the pile. He read it and would like to do it."

After that we are both excited, because one of the men walking down the road in the synchronized story is going to find his way into the world, and secretly we feel that this gives the other man in the short story some hope for his own realization. The Journalist is like the fond parent in this triangle, which disturbs me immensely. I have the desire to follow The African Literature Guy home when he says goodbye. I think of him, preparing lectures in a bohemian flat which smells of youth. I want to uncover his life, his war. I think of his artistic hands when they were even younger- I try to imagine them forced to cradle a heavy FN automatic rifle for two years, or holding the broken head of a dying man as he tried to breathe life into cold, black lips.

In the night I hold The Journalist fiercely, blinding myself to the pain as I tell him, love me.

Apartheid made life simple, polemic. Everything that was bad and evil emanated from the white racist government. The ANC was the recipient of all our sympathy. In Johannesburg the young white baby-faced police force was often on campus with teargas and rubber bullets, playing hide-and-seek with the students, synonymous to them with communists and terrorists. Sometimes I accompanied the African Literature Guy to the local jail to bail out arrested students and give them a ride home.

The African Literature Guy has strong hands, which demand my attention. They give him away. I see a strength there that is not in his face or his voice. I see someone who has been buried. I try to dig him up, feeling strong, large.

I only see The Journalist at night, and like it when the lights are out. Then I listen to his voice; it is warm and strong. I don't breathe in his smell or touch the sagging skin at his neck. Any terror of death or time is hidden under my skin. One day the terror begins to erupt. At twenty I have a face full of acne. It stays with me for years, after Africa, after The Journalist.

I write this book from an obscure place along the journey. The narrative does not develop in a linear fashion.

I look back from a place in California, in a small café where I work for five dollars an hour. Before sunrise the streets of the Californian coastal town are wet. Men in overalls hose down the debris, the broken bottles and grotty remnants of Saturday night. In the café, I begin making the first cappuccino. I pour the white bubbles of milk foam into the muddy espresso, and stir it in, leaving golden streaks and trails through the foam. I am caught in an image of golden waving grasses in a place and time far from this one.

When the Beach Police come in for coffee I retreat to the back of the store and let someone else serve them. I am the Girl with the British accent. People think I am about sixteen. I tell some of them that I'm twenty-five and not from England at all.

Vivid images from my life begin after all this time, to emerge in the milk. I can hardly believe what I am doing; can hardly comprehend that every captured image in my life was a step towards this one. There are two books published, and others written, but I've had no luck for years and have become despondent. I have always kept a journal, recording events so that nothing would remain uncaptured.

A second set of images emerges now when I am twenty-five. As I work these hours in the café, everything that I didn't write, that I didn't capture in my image cavern, stirs up and floats to the surface of the milk that I am busy steaming. I had no vision of myself in this position. I am beginning to see that I have been ignorant, that I thought I was able to consciously contain every event that I have ever been part of. Ignorant is the word, which now clings to me, as I try to emerge from an old skin.

I went with The African Literature Guy to Zimbabwe. I left The Journalist behind and told him not to worry, that I loved him.

The Zimbabwe Ruins coil around in ancient circles. They are the site of controversy both political and spiritual. There are myths of Solomon's Mines, of the Queen of Sheba. There are echoes of riches, of a great mystery just hovering above the fertile green hills. Voices carry across the granite and green for miles. The figures that walk through the ruins that day after a thunderstorm feel small and insignificant in the face of such grandeur.

The African Literature Guy has grown in size. Now his face has the strength of his hands. He is a musician. The Angel of Common Sense that The Journalist has requested breathes into my ear the first night I am in Zimbabwe, without him. I wake to the sound of tropical birds whose notes hang like suspended raindrops above my head. I look at the white brick wall. At the fat spider on the ceiling. I see an immeasurable tragedy. I picture myself with children. I will still have no money and be with The Journalist and he will have no money. I will never see anything else, but live in South Africa and walk strollers over bloodstained streets in the morning.

I meet some Zimbabweans, walk the streets of Harare, see the beggars, the starving children on the doorsteps of shops. I feel the legacy of too much blood spilled on the ground that we stroll over so lightly. My heart breaks because my powerlessness is unbearable. My love for Africa deepens; my hate of any sort of human degradation increases.

The African Literature Guy walks along low brick walls and balances across fallen trees. We go rock-climbing and explore caves. We allow the Nyangombe river to carry us on a rushing muddy journey into a deep rock pool where we swim against the current to get to the side. We hide from torrential rain beneath the narrow eaves of a curio shop, watching as the road turns into a river of iron oxide-red mud. I feel young. I realize for the first time in my life that I am young. For the first time I let myself remember the wrinkles, smell the smell of The Journalist's forty-something years against my twenty, recall how my body contracts and goes small.

The African Literature Guy plays me his music. We climb a huge tree and go to the Balancing Rocks. We whisper across the granite and listen to each other's voices carried over a huge distance. We walk along African dirt roads in the heat of the day as lonely pick-up trucks speed by, and become two characters in the same story. His arm brushes mine once and I am dizzy. He grows larger, and I make myself small lest I frighten him away.

It was the act of making myself small that was the hardest to undo.

The book is eventually accepted by the publisher, but there is no formal contract. Doubt sets in and eventually it is the same as before. The publisher avoids me. I try to contact him but he is always engaged in some matter of huge importance.

The Journalist's close friend is the journalist who knows about me. One day I hear that the friend has been killed not far from his township home, shot in the head at close range. I hear that someone strolled up behind him as he walked home from the taxi rank, and called his name. He turned to see who it was.

I tell the African Literature Guy that I am sick and tired of South Africa, of the fear and the violence. He listens to me, and invites me to one of his lectures, and to hear his band play. In the lecture hall there are over a hundred faces of mixed races and ages. They listen and suddenly he has a strong voice and projects it up over the rows of seats. I hear the discussion as if I am far up in the sky. I see the lecturer, but also the boy with the FN rifle, an emotional casualty of a terrible war. I look down on him but he grows in size and I shrink. I lose definition. A Zulu student stands up after the lecture and announces in both languages that their very own dear lecturer will be playing at the Yard of Ale tonight, and please to come along.

In the smoky room his fingers touch strings and frets and the music goes into my soul and erases the past. I fall in love with the fingers on the guitar, and the weak voice that can turn itself strong in a lecture hall or through a microphone.

Afterwards I go home to The Journalist, smell Honeysuckle in the air, hear thunder, the first sign of spring. I say to myself that my life is impossible. He is possessive. He says he wants to own me, have me, but I no longer feel flattered by this, and squirm away, leaving him staring up at the ceiling in the house where he lives.

*

Sometimes, from this place in California, I think of him. He lives out his life on the other side of the world in Africa. He is older now, and his hair is white. I think of the hands that held my head and the feverish lips that clung to mine. I think of drinking hot chocolate with him late at night in the gold Toyota when I told him I no longer wanted to be with him. I said I would throw myself at the first man who presented himself to me, because I was old before my time and wanted to live a young life. I think of how he said: "Be careful to whom you give yourself —you are infinitely precious." How I felt the full impact of his love, was filled with derision for what I was about to do, and did it anyway.

Now, life is not a continuous series of new and different possibilities, rather the same elements reappearing in different forms. I feel great sadness for him, for his loss. I understand his heart, as I always did.

I went to The African Literature Guy's flat in Yeoville. He was surprised to see me, and we went out together to eat pizza. I drank too much and we walked down Rockey Street, looking on at the tacky neon lights, at the homeless children sleeping in the doorways of *Dylan's* and *African Magic*. We passed a man standing in an alley. The blood that ran down his face was black and shiny, and his eyes rested on us silently as we walked away.

In the flat he put on a yellow kettle and made tea. We talked about African Writers and the economy, the cost of sending a manuscript and how one might not, because of economics and politics, get published anymore by this or that particular publisher.

"It's probably immoral anyway to sit around writing books while the entire continent is facing starvation," I said. "No one can afford books. No wonder really, that publishers are going bankrupt."

"In America you can do writing at university. You can do an entire degree in Creative Writing," he said. "There is a context in society, where writers can safely exist. Look, an application form for a doctoral degree there." He showed me a letter on rich, silky paper that exuded a First World aura. He held it to my nose so that I could smell the paper and the dark laser print. I breathed in deeply. I felt the drunkenness in my head merge with the throbbing crickets outside. His hands covered my breasts and the night swallowed me whole, for the first time, without pain, without regret, as I became the tide and washed us both out to sea.

The morning that followed was the same as the night before. It repeated itself over several days. I took such pleasure in the disembodied self which I had become, that I no longer cared that he had grown immense, filling an entire universe, and I relinquished all size and dimension, existing only as an instrument on which he played.

⌇

I am finished with the second book. It is accepted and published immediately. We go to Cape Town, where the book is set, to meet the publishers. We see the jeweled city at the edge of the sea, and say we are here from the future, looking at our small, as yet unfulfilled selves in Africa, before we know what will happen to us. We are full of hope. We do not sense then, unbearable winters, an icy wind that betrays trees, the loss of vast, folded mountain ranges.

The act of this projection into the future back into the present as past sets me adrift. I miss The Journalist but I no longer want to be with him. I want to tell him about my new life, about my book, about the love.

All night, every night we lie in bed; we are wet and slippery, eels in a shimmering ocean that is silent. It is always silent. I ache to hear words, but there are never any. Some mornings before he wakes up, I look at his face, gentle and smooth in sleep, hands folded quietly over his chest. He does not dream of war. He is so young. He smells like washing powder and the warmth of beds that are slept in. I contrast this. I compare it. I look at myself then and now, and in the future. I cry, but he never sees it. When he opens his eyes I am there.

As soon as the second book was published, the editor at the small press sent me the contract for the first. It just arrived in a heavy brown envelope.

At the café where I work in California, I can watch the sea from the window. I love the expanse of blue, it reminds me of deep African skies. After the first two years in America spent in a cold northern climate near Chicago, I am relieved to wake to skies that are open, that do not press down their gray somberness and bury you beneath the weight of hundreds of unhappy generations.

There is a customer who knows that I write. He read my book and asked if it was true. I said yes, some of it is. He said: "I didn't know that there were poor whites in South Africa."

The job requires that I stand for nine hours during the day. I have begun to notice that there are veins breaking near my knees and thighs. I do not know what to do about these spidery red and purple threads which should not be there.

Sometimes I think of suicide, but I know I will not do it. I would try to rescue myself because I am too desperate to make this life have meaning.

After it is rumored that Nelson Mandela will soon be released from prison, South Africa is euphoric. I am just finishing my degree. The transformation fought for at university, in the streets, in homes and lives, through wars, is at hand. The South African President, F.W De Klerk, a balding dyed-in-the-wool Afrikaaner, is of a new and different breed. He has plans to negotiate himself out of power, and there is cause for hope and optimism. But the beggar who sat bent over on the corner of Jan Smuts Avenue and Jorrissen street, with his hand held up to the sky, is there still. The children in their rags who once broke the skin on my hand as I offered them a coin, are still there. And there is death everywhere. There are bullets and knife wounds, and high walls with broken glass around the rich homes in Hyde Park and Sandton. There are thirty thousand deaths from violent crime in a single year. "I'm leaving this place," I say.

I was the girl in class who always had a cold. I never breathed through my nose. My mouth was constantly open. The one with the mucousy voice who was teased however hard she tried to be like the others. "I'm sorry," she would say if she bumped someone's desk, and they would smirk. "Oops," she'd say as she tripped over a foot deliberately stuck out from under another desk. She'd smile at the sniggers, try to merge with the class spirit. But she was set apart because her parents were not rich enough to buy her a new tennis racket. The one she had was bought for two Rand from another girl in the class. There was a hole in the racket, which could not be fixed, and to top it all, the racket was warped. "Sorry," she said on the court to the harsh voice of the tennis instructor. "Missed again."

"Move those legs," the instructor shouted, and so she would run, wiping her nose, wiping it and wiping it as it dripped so that she could not see – felt only the burning green floor of the court and the harsh sun at its zenith in the eternally deep sky.

It was hardly surprising then that she began to write. Furiously. And it was hardly remarkable that she fell in love, became obsessed with a man more than twice her age, who had once been a prominent journalist for the Star's Africa News Service. What was surprising and astonishing to her, was that the journalist himself became obsessed. That the girl with the infected sinuses could become a symbol of lust and desire, an image of femininity, a fantasy of perfection in these older, piercing eyes. That was as jarring as Salvador Dali's *Persistence of Memory*. What emerged suddenly through this mutual obsession was not simply obscene. The school art classes were studying the sculptures of Henry Moore; the relation of the feminine form to nature and the symbolism of Mother Earth. Brancusi's *KISS*, Rodin's *KISS*—the Girl with the Blocked Nose was at once transformed. The art teacher recommended a career in Fine Arts, but she refused then, the girl of seventeen, being aware exclusively and all the time of The Journalist, and the Kiss that waited behind the silence of the written word.

The letters written to The Journalist carried a burden. Every word was an act of consequence. And so it was that *she* found out; and then he told her about me —he told her about being in love with a girl who couldn't breathe unless her mouth was open.

☙

The significance of certain moments up until now only becomes significant in retrospect. It is quite unusual for me to understand the importance of a moment in time as it is being lived. The last time we made love was before I left for Zimbabwe. I thought, I wonder if this is the last time.

Then after that there were the hands of The African Literature Guy.

The boy I loved when we were children died when he was twenty-six, but he is always a boy to me. I dream that I am nine years old. We are riding our bikes down some paved drive. There are cirrus clouds in the sky and tall oak trees, and the smell of pine and jasmine. There are two bikes, men's bikes. I am too small to ride my bike, so I have to stretch my leg beneath the cross-bar and can only coast down the hill, popping the purple jacaranda blossoms that lie scattered on our path, before I walk the bike up again. My friend can ride the bike he has, because his legs are long for his age. He teases me that I have scars on my legs and that I'm catching flies again, standing there with my mouth open. Suddenly I wake up from this dream. I can hardly believe that I am not nine. I am shocked, think that he is really DEAD. Then I get up quietly and go into the kitchen. On the fridge there is a magnet: *Domino's Pizza.* And an ad: *SUBS for half price.* I think: I now live in this strange place where they have things called SUBS.

There is the possibility that I am just one of several million in self-imposed exile; that I am an element of a universal cliché.

In South Africa for a long time literature was prescriptive. It had to further the struggle, ally itself with the cause. Writers were obliged to use their talents to express the suffering of the oppressed masses. There was very little distinction (or this was the hope) between literature by South Africans, and journalism by South Africans. He was The Journalist, and I made him the hero of my story.

I met someone who thought recently that I had to be independently wealthy in order to have come so far across the world. I said to him, either that, or the complete opposite.

It is believed by some that the true feminist text should not develop in a linear fashion, but should unfold, layer by layer, should be cyclical. I try to imagine myself writing to a prescription.

*

I no longer defend any ideology. Even my own. If it exists. I think though, of the linear as opposed to the cyclical. A body travelling in one direction in a linear fashion eventually returns to the beginning. It is the belief in the existence of the linear that appears to be the fallacy.

*

I looked at her, at her long brown hair, felt her cheek against mine and smelt her warmth. She was my goddess. I was in love with her. My mother. Her arms were around me and I loved to be hers. I sat in the grass knowing how I was the baby, hers, myself. The split-pole fence was brown and when the people walked by talking their African languages, I could see the bright colors of their blankets and beads behind the slats of wood.

*

There were other goddesses: the teacher whose heels clicked down the slasto corridors of the school, whose perfume preceded the afternoon thundershowers; the friend whose mannerisms were addictive. Her small wrist flicking the hair out of her eye made the onlooker envious of that action, to such a point that it was agony to not be that person, to not be the one with the slim wrist flicking soft, straight, golden hair. The only remedy for the pain that this beauty caused, was to get as close to it as possible; to share secrets, borrow clothes and stand skin to skin in the shower. There were no words to be found for this kind of love.

When we were eleven, the girl whose mannerisms I loved, followed me up the river near our house. We jumped over the water, stepping on rocks, not wanting to get Bilharzia. The river had been in flood, and the air was heavy with a terrible rotten odor. We came upon a tree stump covered in wet grass and river slime. As we peered into the slime we saw a gray-brown doll. Sand filled the open mouth and deep eye sockets. Then there was the umbilical cord still attached, and we understood the smell. A baby? Had a mother, desperate in ways we could not fathom, thrown the baby from the bridge further along the river? Had it been alive? Maybe it was dead already. Had the river swept by a hut somewhere upstream, carrying a sleeping newborn baby with it?

The police arrived. They carried a black garbage bag. They picked up the little body, and flicked it head-over-heels into the bag, so that the two small ebony feet banged together.

God had created the world according to males. There was anger when the girl of eleven had to stop being a child. The girl wished fervently that she had been born a boy, vowed revenge on the world for the body, which now began to be pulled like other bodies of water, by the moon. When there was no answer from the universe, she stopped eating, starved herself until her ribs showed, until her hair grew thinner and thinner, until the mother whom she loved so much grew pale and concerned and said to the girl that she would do lasting damage to her body if she continued this. The girl tried, listened, wanted to heal. She watched the rains nourishing the red earth, felt the seasons of dryness and moisture, tried to understand that fertility was not very different from these cycles.

One day, these fertile cycles will end. I think of the girl whose manner I loved, whose face I will always love, and of the teacher, who has grown old in the time that I have been away from Africa. Her voice is harder, though not by choice. I do not love her any less than I did at the very beginning. I begin to think that women don't carry the burden of the world on their shoulders as I thought when I was younger. I think of them as having a key, of a lock in the universe waiting to be opened. Birth is possibly the secret to death. The passage is similar, I start to think.

Most of the time I feel my existence as small and fragile. Sometimes I emerge, and it's like this: I stand looking at the horizon where the sun sets. The light vanishes over the edge of the world and in my smallness I don't see beyond that. Even though I am conscious that it is the earth that is turning, and that the sun is not literally setting, I can only step out of this reality very briefly. For me it grows dark and the sun is swallowed. If I were a million miles tall and wide, I would see how the light is constant, would see how the flat horizon is the curve of a sphere, would feel the earth turning.

I go to visit the person I call The African Literature Guy. I let myself into the Yeoville flat. He is not there. It is raining, spring in the Transvaal. The cat purrs against my leg. Unable to believe the code of trust I am breaking, I look into the diary, which lies open on his bed. There I find that he is in love with someone else. A poem has been written recently, to someone else. I close the book and look at the rain. Then I cry onto the cat.

South Africa is like this: rolling savanna, baobab trees and granite mountains, turquoise ocean and purple jacaranda streets; criminals —a lost generation of armed youths trained for a revolution, which looks more and more like it isn't going to come; beggars, destitute children; a sprawling city crawling with flies, poverty and suffering. It becomes overwhelming, the poverty and suffering. I begin to hate everything because of the cars that are hijacked and the occupants killed. I hate the beauty, and the silent, inactive God. You see then that you are powerless, or possibly all-powerful. You no longer know whose story you are telling.

You can stay with the person who worships you, to whom you are everything, who sees the universe in your head and feels you infinitely precious. Or you can follow the injured person whose hands wring your heart, who superimposes a smaller self onto your reality, who is partially blind to the true person you are, whose breath in and out is the pulse of all life; whose story begins in the exact same way that yours does.

I was in love before we made love. It was when he took his clothes off, and he was beautiful to look at. I touched him, tasted him. He lay down and I couldn't stop myself. The night was raw and outside the Yeoville flat some street children were breaking bottles on the pavement before they would break into a car, possibly mine, but I didn't care. Thought nothing of my things, even my life, only of the slippery body that strained towards me. When we made love, there were tears but no pain —the thunderstorm after a drought, my desire hovering over us in the room.

*

I love him from that night onwards. He goes to sleep with his arms around me, says softly first that he has a glass plate over his heart —I must not be broken by him.

*

The journalist who was killed was a man who wrote about education. About Spirit and Individualism. He was killed for his words. I could not exist anymore in a place where people died for their words. I wanted to be free, to not be caught in the trap of censoring everything, even unconsciously, because of fear.

I can't continue any longer in a place where it is not believed that a writer may write beyond the self.

*

So this is how it can happen that you stop seeing the beauty that does in fact exist, that you close yourself to the majesty and mystery of an ancient, though blood-soaked continent. It also had to do with money, and violence. You lose sight of everything that you once loved, people, places. You detest the smells, focus only on the economy, on how the price of bread doubles every ten days, on how you cannot get any kind of decent job, and nor can ten million others your age. It's too dangerous to drive or walk. You see someone shot. Someone stabbed. You think anywhere in America is at least better because of the economy.

I never look at his diary again. I never tell him what I have read. He seems to know. We talk about leaving Africa together, think of ways to get into other countries. If we were married, it would be easier, since my passport at this time is prohibitive.

I finely attuned myself to his sensitive fingers. I was the girl who became the guitar so that he could play as he wanted, up and down the frets, the girl who bent her body so that it became an arc of pleasure, a waterfall of lust, desire, madness —because through the softness of his skin she could feel the glass, the barrier.

A long-haired blonde goddess begins to haunt her dreams, strangling her in gossamer threads of gold. He loved this essence, with all of himself, and so she, the girl who makes herself into a guitar, loves the goddess too, relinquishes her own desire to be seen because the light blinding his eyes is far too near. In her dreams she follows him as he makes love to his goddess. She becomes him, and loves the goddess with him.

He doesn't want to cause her pain, he says, and she feels she could die, the pain is so great. She walks the Yeoville streets, seeks out the goddess in a jazz club, and watches her all afternoon, thinking, this, he loves, this hair, these hands, the mouth that holds a cigarette. She listens to the African jazz, resisting the cacophony of sounds, the loudness. She sees that the goddess has hardly any breasts, that her body is large and overwhelming. She daydreams of touching those breasts, the hair, her thighs, or, of what it feels like to look out at the world through a long golden curtain.

Then she goes back to the Yeoville flat and makes love to him in an exasperated wish to annihilate whatever image he has superimposed over her.

You no longer believe in Time as going beyond the small sphere of earth. But you are bound by its rules here, and so you are compelled to act out your life according to some vast illusion of linear Progression.

♌

I am haunted by the figure of my real father. I see myself in the shadow of his walk, which is the walk of someone bent over by an invisible burden. In South Africa, he runs a small business. His pharmacy is where poor people go to get free medical advice. He is a gentle and compassionate character. One night he is suddenly arrested and taken to the main prison, thrown in side by side with hard core criminals. His crime is that he is in debt. The young white policeman who handcuffs the aging pharmacist says viciously, now we will teach these Jews a lesson.

My father sleeps with his wedding ring in his mouth for several endless days, so that his fingers don't get chopped off. I know he does not really sleep at all. Later on I learn about the assault. No one can understand how such a terrible thing could happen to him, of all people. Afterwards, he is released and everything is smoothed over. "It was simply a misunderstanding," I hear. Or, "It should never have gone this way." But his voice has permanently changed. It trembles like an old man's as he tells me that in this archaic system, you are guilty until you can prove your innocence.

I want to throw myself across the world as an anchor, root myself in the Land of Opportunity, and pull the people who wish to come, across the Atlantic. I want to live in a place where you can declare yourself bankrupt and start again, instead of going to jail.

The goddess comes back to me. She has many faces. I see her everywhere. She blots me out on the streets in cafés, on the covers of magazines. She seems to exist everywhere but in me. The plate of glass is dark, and I am eclipsed.

The girl who left Africa did not know what a dichotomy she carried with her. She did not realize what a paradox she was, how inescapable it was. In Europe, for the first time she found herself amongst more white people than black. She was part of a majority, treated as one of Them. Then, being white and from South Africa, there were more images attached to her than she could dissolve. She could not escape being white and from South Africa. She was most at home talking to a Ghanaian woman.

There is something blocking me from view, and I cannot remove it.

⚘

The African Literature Guy is originally from Zimbabwe. He is more recognizably African wherever we go.

⚘

Two days after we got married, we left South Africa. My second book had just been released. I did not marry him for any other reason but that I loved him and I wanted to be with him. He married me because he did not want to leave the person whose story was his own, whom he would never find again if he lost. I hated the ceremony in the courthouse in Johannesburg where the man in the overall who was next in line, had come to report the death of his brother, shot in the head. I thought of clear mountain streams and the voices of the singers from the African Pentecostal church, and I had the first inkling of homesickness, of how I was blinding myself.

⚘

I think of the diary entry when I was seventeen: "I haven't done anything of value in the world, after seventeen years of being in it." I think I am grateful to the universe for blinding me to the future, and leaving me with a pattern, a map in my soul, which I follow without seeing clearly sometimes, trying to feel my way.

I start to believe that a cliché is the superficial interpretation of a deep pattern in the universe.

I have taken on the task of unraveling clichés, so that what underlies them can be looked at with discernment. I unravel the pattern of The Journalist and me, and I get tangled in the unraveling. The threads have no end.

Before The Journalist's hair went completely white, before everything, there was the picture of a tragedy. I saw myself coming back to see him years later, being with someone else. I saw how whether we became entangled in a relationship or not, there would never be any resolution.

I find my true self in a dream of the Africa I once knew. I am far from it now, but not as far as I have believed up until this point, the present.

You stand there, on land that is rich and fertile, you smell the moist earth, the plants. Banking on the southwestern horizons in the afternoons, thunderclouds promise rain. The drops that come down are hard and heavy, they thunder onto the iron roofs, the grass roofs, they carve dongas in the soft sand. You are small, you are in danger, but you have no limits. If you allow yourself, you can expand across the whole landscape. You can stand on this hill and see for three hundred or more kilometers. This is where you take stock of your life, see how from this height your life, the idea of time in which you live, evaporates like morning fog in the sun. Your struggle for survival seems like a small bump on a far away sand road. And you have left this place, are free to return to it now only in dreams.

You think of the man whom you met on the Zimbabwe mountain, and the moment which you recognized as significant as it passed.

The man was as brown as the earth, and he climbed barefoot over the rocks. He told you he had gone up the mountain to pray. He told you he was twenty years old. That he had never been anywhere except this part of Africa. That he knew this was the most beautiful place in the world. That you were not really safe on the mountain because of baboons and lions. He asked you where you were staying.

The next day he left you a bag of rich, sweet, ripe mangoes from one of his own trees. His name was Jasper. You never saw him again.

If life is some journey from which each one of us is reluctantly plucked at some point along the way, then I will make my journey meaningful. I have seen lives which end too suddenly, and so I decide that each day must be full and rich, so that I am never unresolved or unfulfilled. And this task I set myself is bittersweet, because it causes the ache for fulfillment to widen until I feel madness set in.

I told The Journalist over the phone about the marriage.

"Are you in love?" he asked me. I talked about the cheap flights to Luxembourg and how it was not that difficult to find a way to England once already in Europe. I said I had my heart set on America. I stared out of a window into a sky, which had once been filled with the shape of The Journalist's face.

The last time I see The Journalist, we sit in a garden. The house is older, walls are stained with time and brown water marks. The small brothers have grown older. The fig-tree is now so tall it covers my old bedroom window from sight. The grass is wild and it is three years since we first made love, and nine years that he has loved me. His smile has cracked and broken, and hovers in pieces over his face. I sit next to him, as still as stagnant water, and hear how his tears slide down his cheeks into his mouth. His arm wants to touch me, but he lets it fall in the grass. I think of how I once wrote: one day I will fall in love with someone else.

He says to me that he will always love me, in the way that he loves me, and it is then that I see the immensity of the sadness, which we did nothing to avoid. I ask him:

"Would you ever go back to her?"

"No, I could never."

*

I am always conscious of my mortality. In every word I write there is the consciousness of my own birth and death.

*

At first, when we leave Africa we travel through Europe. We think it will be easier to get to America from England because then we won't be seen as Third World Refugees looking for an excuse to be in the Land of Opportunity —which is how we feel. In London we see musicians on the streets, comedians, watch jugglers in Covent Garden. He is distant and disturbed for a lot of the time. He keeps saying, "we married because we wanted to be with each other, but I don't see myself as married." He feels sorry for The Journalist, for his loss. He tells me repeatedly that the reason for the glass plate over his heart is because of the one who left golden gossamer threads of her hair in his carpet in Yeoville when she went away. I try to imagine the memories of someone with artistic hands who learns to operate an FN rifle; who, at eighteen risked his life by refusing to shoot into huts during a war-time village sweep-through, because, he thought, there might be children in there.

Knowing what he loves, I chart the passage of certain women who fit an invisible mould. I am sexually aroused by them, as I imagine he would be. I live into the way they smile, the fall of blonde hair over shoulders. I live in a shell, hiding. I grow into the shell until I am small enough. I am once again clumsy, the girl with infected sinuses who bangs herself on doors and catches her toes on the legs of chairs.

I write to my mother. I send photographs of Europe to my stepfather and brothers. I never write to my father. I did not even phone him to say that I was leaving. I think of him as we walk to catch the tube from Finsbury Park to Covent Garden, over wet, spring London streets.

I begin to develop a habit of generalizing. I make one sweeping generalization. It is that foreigners are ignorant about Africa.

I think about why we married, and about why it is that people usually marry. The African Literature Guy tells me that when he was younger he had a nightmare that recurred. In the dream there were two moths. The one was alive, and the other, dead. The living moth was trying to carry the dead moth across the window sill, struggling against the weight that held him back. The African Literature Guy tells me he was always terrified of being tied to a dead moth.

All that I write up until this point is what rises to the surface of the milk as I steam it in this beach town in California.

The writing is the act of undoing the crime.

I travel to the foot of a mountain, which exists in a memory. I am almost thirteen. I am walking through tall elephant grass, following my mother and stepfather. They carry the boys who are too tired to walk any more. We are looking for a picnic spot along the river. I've seen thunderclouds, indigo-black on the horizon. All the while we are walking I am complaining that we should not be going this far because of the storm. I threaten them with lightning, with the river in flood. They are humorous and unaffected by my anxiety, which in turn angers me. I fail to see the way the grass catches the gold of the sun while the rest of the sky goes dark. I don't hear the rushing river, the warm chatter of parents. The mountain is in the shadow of the cloud. It takes half an hour for the storm to close in. We are caught in

the first heavy soaking drops of rain, and all I think about, is
how I was right.

＊

The sound of the steamer, which is attached to the cappuccino
machine, is deafening and although the milk should not be
hotter than a hundred and fifty degrees Fahrenheit, I boil it to
one eighty. It spills over my hand, burning me. I see a life being
lived, which does not feel like mine. I transplant myself back to
the foot of the mountain, and listen to the thunder, to the water
over rocks, to the sound of voices that are loved. It fragments
in the froth on top of the double cappuccino, the wide open
spaces, the silent brick houses where I had never heard of
earplugs —and didn't know what they looked like. Where it was
so quiet you could hear a snake sliding over the kitchen floor in
the middle of the night.

＊

Before The Journalist, there was the friend who lived on a
farm at whose house we would have parties every weekend. The
house was stone and thatch. The friend had horses which were
kept in the paddock at the bottom of the huge property, next
to the mountain of rocks known as the Kopje. The swimming

pool was green, and we jumped naked from a ledge into the water, and stayed there in summer ecstasy until the afternoon thunderstorms threatened lightning. We took the horses and rode bare back out of the property down to a river. After wading the animals through, we came to an island of river sand and willow trees. We tethered the horses to a willow and trailed our hands in the river, not mentioning Bilharzia, waiting for the sun to set, hearing only the stomp of hooves and the tearing of clumps of grass from beneath the trees.

We promised one another in our innocence on the riverbank that when we grew older we would be exactly the same as we were then.

Not long after this, there was The Journalist who grew up in Zimbabwe, when it was Rhodesia, just like the African Literature Guy did eighteen years later.

In the London summer, we stay in a tiny brick house with relatives and sleep on a sofa-bed in the lounge. It is there that the person I love falls ill. For a while we don't know the cause of such a raging fever. When yellow blisters appear on his skin, in his eyes and mouth, it is diagnosed as a childhood disease, dangerous to adults. We have nowhere else to go. Outside, the undergrowth tangles itself around the window-ledges, and birds sing songs that I have never heard before. One night, when his fever shows no sign of subsiding and he has begun to smell foreign and look unrecognizable, he says that he feels he might die. His body is so hot that I sleep on the floor, breathing in dog-hairs as I will him to recover, make deals with the universe.

After weeks like this, he emerges thin and scarred. I have won. He says he loves me, that one of the layers between us has been burnt away.

For some time after this the goddesses are absent from my dreams.

You find yourself, after Europe and the struggle to get a visa, in Wisconsin, North America. Summer is the noise of machines humming and hacking, trees being sawn down and pruned, roads being fixed. There is the constant clatter of machinery; the sounds rip through the air and leave it in tatters. The small houses are packed tightly together, and inside, huge people hide sadly behind closed shutters, waiting for relief from this brief heat, waiting for when the icy blasts of winter force everyone into an eight month hibernation. Winter is a holocaust of cold, a malicious cold that obliterates any senses; no smells exist at all, no colors but white and gray, and no sound but the noise of the machines, the garbage trucks and snow-plows. I feel there, as if a million buckets of lead flowed though my veins. Feel no joy. As if beauty no longer exists in the world. As if you caused the problem initially by being blind to it in the first place —as if Wisconsin is the result of not perceiving the essence of Africa.

🦌

We are in the middle of the Midwest, North America because there is a doctoral program in English. We have come here for him, so that he can study, so that we have an excuse for being in America. We come straight from London, having waited, holding our breath for the visas that will allow us finally into the Land of Opportunity. I am twenty- three.

The houses lining the roads look like those of Eastern Europe. There is no space; everything is piled on top of everything else like a huge junk-heap. Everything is old. Gray. The sky is white and humid. I try to breathe but my chest won't let me. I look around in disappointment. This is not America! I meet someone who says: this place is like Germany would have been if Hitler had won the war.

Such words would not be appreciated by the people who live there.

I am caught by the vision of my mother as I left her:

"If you leave out of such antipathy you could find yourself in a worse position in America than you are here."

Never, I said.

"You could find yourself looking back with regret at a decision made in such anger."

Not ever, I said.

"I'll always be here for you, if you need anything."

I want to go and live in America, and have lots of money, be so rich that I can help you all, and then I want you to come over too.

"I love being in Africa. I love what I do. I don't need to be rescued."

From this present distance, the love the daughter feels for the mother is so strong, that she cannot bear the idea of having argued with her, of having thought herself clearer, even about her own life.

It is in the Midwest, after two years of bleak seasons and isolation, that her heart is broken, and she fades to nothing, having seen the pattern from the beginning. So she cries for her mother.

The Midwest is the place of crises, the antithesis of Africa. It becomes an entity on which one wishes to wreak havoc, destroy. It is an emblem of futility, of how distant the human race has grown from its initial habitation of the earth. A girl sits in an apartment listening to cracking wood boards under heavy footsteps overhead. She sits there without moving —a rat in a cage. Outside the wind is blowing. Bitter temperatures. A church bell rings. The windows have iced over inside and the air is stale. The same air that smelled rotten and fermented in summer is recycled through the heating system three months later. It is in the dim light of early afternoon, that she recalls the brilliance of a sun that shines from directly overhead onto lush luminous green. She recalls the spacious sky, the stark black shadows cast after midday, and the smell and sound of early African dawn. The memory of this beauty is unbearable. So she tries to bury it. While waiting for the man she has married to return from his American class in Creative Writing, she tries unsuccessfully to banish Africa from her heart.

⟼

In my dreams I traverse two landscapes. I am caught between them. The first is an expanse of white sands and turquoise sea. The warmth of the sun is evident on my back. The light is so bright that I have to squint. It is like Cape Town in Africa. All the time I am aware that the reality is different. That I have left Cape Town, and now live in a cold North American town on the banks of Lake Michigan. In the other half of the landscape, the sand turns to snow. The cold is painful. My heart aches for the warmth that it has just left behind. I have a foot on each of these two whites. When I wake from this dream I find myself in the middle of the Midwest in America. I am twenty-three, and there is someone next to me in the bed.

❧

He is concerned and withdrawn because she appears to have gone mad. She bangs her fists against the paper-thin walls and hurls abuse out into the freezing rain. She is starving, and won't eat. She can't breathe and he feels it as a terrible burden. He wishes he had come alone to America. His nightmare of the moth returns. They never sleep because of Concrete Feet upstairs who neurotically paces her rooms until midnight, and then again at five in the morning. They no longer make love.

❧

I look at this picture without judgement. The madness was the pain of having come to believe in my crushed self —the act that rendered me invisible.

I try to become a writer in America. I am sure that this is why I am here. I submit things everywhere. I discover that I am one of a million struggling, invisible writers. I suffer from making too many stylistic errors, and certainly there is Something Not Right with my Point of View. I find myself in an artistic landscape, which is as desolate as the physical one.

I thought that America was the place.

The ghost of the past comes around again and tells me that the reason I left Africa was because I could not write without having to incorporate the beggar on the corner of Jan Smuts Avenue and Jorissen Street who sat there with his hand held up to the sky. The ghost makes me aware of how impossible it was to ignore the suffering, the women fighting with broken bottles in the road at sunset, the children who were hungry. And then I start to think that all that is right, and that I should not be ignoring suffering, that to feel it is to be human, and to escape it is to cause this present blandness, this absence of life and color, this madness of Nothingness, of sterility, and Not Being Seen.

Let me look at the beggar, see his gangrenous foot, his white hair and pitch black skin. Imagine that he grew up in the mountains, that he did not imagine his life ending, some eighty years later, in a filthy street leading to a gigantic city. His body is curved and shaped like Humility. When I put two Rand in his hand, he does not look up and I wonder if he has seen me go past every day for two years.

And so in the bleak, Midwestern winter, I allow the pain to start creeping out for the beggar fourteen thousand kilometers away, two years back in time, without being devoured by my own selfish sense of helplessness.

This is not the equivalent of the White Man's Burden.

Because I am a white African, I can never have an Authentic Voice.

Winter continues endlessly. My skin turns so pale that I see the blue veins in my arms and legs. I look out at the cracked streets, listen to the snow-blowers. The snow stays white for the first day, and then turns gray and black with all the pollution. I meet some people in the English Department. They don't know that the African Literature Guy has a wife. Then they think it is all right that a wife stays at home in a Winter Box.

I am stunned by the recurrence of Not Being Seen. I am superseded, trodden on by mundane, narrow feet. I am in shadow, unable to speak, to be heard. I fall into the abyss. I am unseeable.

✍

I enjoy the Things America has to offer. For a while. I can buy a car if I want to, for eight hundred dollars. I can copy manuscripts for five cents a page. I can speak on the phone to Africa for one dollar a minute.

I can't smell anything.
Or see anything.
Noise has polluted my mind and the story fragments.
For a long time there is absolutely nothing to say.

✍

There is the dream of Cape Point and the wind that whips your hair into a spiral. You are standing at the end of the world. The blues of the two colliding currents, the Indian and Atlantic Ocean, wind around each other. The white foam frames the base of the mountain, and the smell of mountain herbs is the smell of the whole spirit of the place. You are held there as if by a spell, the sensuality is overwhelming, and while you know you must leave this, you are powerless. The wind is a force that you thought spoke to you at night as it howled around your house. It burned you by cooling you so that you did not feel the heat of the midday sun. You believe you have been ravished by the elements — the sea, the in- and outgoing tides, the rain and this wind. And you leave this place.

_

It was also a place of terror, of bloodshed. You left because there was terror in your heart.

_

The goddess dissolved, dissipated. I couldn't find her anymore. She had ceased to haunt me, and her blonde hair had long since untangled from my heart.

_

At first I paid little or no attention to the fact that he, the one who no longer slept with me, began to talk about The Lesbian

Girl more than anything else. He was moved by her love for other women.

*

The small self was so small that at times the person who once existed within a larger idea of itself, couldn't breathe. The doctors sentenced her to using asthmatic sprays, which she hid at the bottom of the medicine cupboard, bargaining with the restriction on her lungs to let her be free.

*

He never said her name to me. He never said my name. Her title was his defense, for my benefit. The love that I had carried so hugely inside me short-circuited. I was not being seen, there was nothing I could do, could say, to change the reality of a thick glass plate that stayed on after the blonde goddess, after the illness in London, after AFTER.

So I try to love where I am. I try to extend myself into my environment. The banks of blue ice on the shores of Lake Michigan, the pale sky and the very distant midday sun. As I look at the small sun, the faraway sun, I cannot help but see it shining down on the equatorial regions, burning the red earth, turning the sea to crystalline blue, casting stark shadows of huge trees against mud hut walls. The beauty and life that the sun bestows are not where I am. They are all on the other side of the world, where I was.

I try to love this place for his sake, so that even if he cannot see me, I'm not only a burden of sadness, something he wishes away. He is kind. He touches my hair as if I were some familiar, small animal. Some afternoons I don't know him at all, and I forget that I wrote books, that in Africa I had perhaps found a voice that I could use, and had stopped it before it had said there, what it needed to say.

The friend who died was a guitarist. The African Literature Guy was a guitarist, but after we get to America, the music dies in him and we sit in silence in the darkest part of the winter.

I have stopped writing to my mother, and to my brothers.

I only want to hear their voices on the phone for a few minutes every month. My mother tells me that The Journalist came to see her. That he told her he misses me, and thinks of me every day.

❧

I am so blind I do not see how she has stepped into my space. How she has slowly eclipsed me. I have never seen her. I walk freezing gray streets and sense my own delusion. He tells me she is a poet, a Poet and a Lesbian. She wears black, thick dark eyeliner, for protection, he says, because some days she feels vulnerable.

❧

I now live in a place where at night you wake with a fright, realizing that you are grown up, no longer nine years old, realizing that there is an advertisement on the fridge for SUBS.

❧

The lake is steel-gray, like a war tank. You walk along the ice. The wind makes your teeth ache; your hands, inside two pairs of gloves, are numb. The sky is a very pale blue, and the trees are leafless and quite black. You feel sorry for them and wish you could give them the experience of a tropical climate where it is not necessary to be without leaves for eight months. It is zero. You have reached absolute zero.

At night I wake from dreams of being suffocated. I can't breathe. I go to the medicine chest and look at the asthma spray. I fight for each breath. It is one in the morning. This life is not mine, the person sitting on the bathroom floor in the yellow light is not me. I drink herbal tea instead. I tell the universe I refuse to attach myself to the can of Ventolin. I think to myself that I would rather be dead than have this for the rest of my life.

We move out from beneath Concrete Feet. At last. It is still winter. Now there are a few more people in the English Department who have heard that the African Literature Guy has a Wife. That she has published books. They do not find it easy to include her, because she looks like a child, and because she has published books, she can't be part of their circle of Struggling Writers.

There was the witchdoctor in Zululand who told people's fortunes in a cave. He sat behind an old car windshield, wearing jeans and a necklace of bones. You could get to him only by climbing up a steep rocky path usually used by mountain goats. Quartz crunched beneath your feet and the mountains stared down at you somberly as you made your way along the path. You passed Bushman paintings on the side of a granite rock but didn't stop because you always passed Bushman paintings in the mountains. You were sixteen.

The array of bones on the floor of the cave was cluttered with other artifacts, doll's legs, broken bottle-tops. I sat on my haunches and smelt the strong smell of the Sangoma. The cave was a huge chamber of rock, a grotto where water dripped down the slimy walls at the back, and turned into a river which rushed out of a hole in the ground outside the cave. The echo of the water was louder than the human voice.

I looked through the car windshield at the man who spat on his palms and rubbed them together. I moved away from him, stood up and walked outside again, listening to the silence, seeing the clouds build castles in the sky on the horizon, leaving the future to the wind.

Before we married and left South Africa, we drove one more time to Zimbabwe. We left in the early hours of the morning. At sunrise, the landscape was a tapestry of acacia trees and hills. The stars in the deepest of night skies, looked like lumps of foil they were so large, until the red rays melted them into the blue of the day. The air was filled with aromas of plants and weeds and animals. We stopped on the strip road in the middle of nowhere, to listen to the sounds of countless birds. This was the closest to love, the closest to truth. The point before the final departure, where everything was clear for a moment.

I think it is fear that stops me from breathing. But I don't know what I am afraid of. I wake at night and try to understand the cause of such a racing pulse. I think maybe it is the lack of light, maybe I have always been a fearful person. Maybe I created the pattern for the disease. So I blame myself for the illness. I encourage myself to feel at fault. But I am not happy with this for long.

I wish for the fears that I used to have, for the veld fire that started near our house in South Africa, scaring me with its huge devouring night flames. For the smell of burned animals and the screech of an owl as the bamboo tree went up in a display of red and blue and orange. I held my mother's hand and watched the men who beat out the flames closest to the house.

The image dissolves. I am back in the winter, afraid of the person next to me in the bed who has turned his back to me and lies there silently.

I imagine the dilemma of women, all women, in the colonies, through all cycles of time. I hope that I am not one of them.

I try to read and write as I love, to uncover what is hidden, like finding the Ultimate Quark in Quantum Physics. But it's so elusive, so secret, moving always, residing for a moment here or there, a moment of epiphany between a reader and words, where the writer collides with a reader, both unaware of a union. The search weakens me, and I begin to disbelieve that there is anything to uncover.

I fear that beneath his glass plate there is a void where a universe used to exist.

I count the months spent in darkness as we descend into another winter. I have cured myself of not being able to breathe. The terror of the winter before has been eliminated. I walk outside in the last days of Fall. I see no beauty in the autumn leaves, I wish that they weren't all dying, the trees and the grass. I inhale deeply, fill my lungs. I will never take another day for granted.

He has apologized for not being able to love me enough, to help me through the illness. I say it is the one thing I have, the knowledge that I cured myself.

In the coldest, darkest winter of our lives, the wind-chill sends temperatures plummeting to seventy below zero. Seventy. I had thought that absolute zero was the bottom, but the depth to which this ink-dark cold could sink, had no limit.

In the darkness, he is under a spell. Her spell. The Lesbian Girl.

It might be that I have already sensed how large she has grown in his vision. Perhaps that is why I write to The Journalist, for the first time in almost two years.

I am haunted by the last night in the gold Toyota where we drank hot chocolate. Now as I write to him I feel properly how the cool night air brushed against my skin. How his tears slipped down onto my arms, and felt cold. How I could have said no, it's a mistake, I don't want to leave you. And instead I sat there, hearing the crickets outside, as something broke inside me and tore away.

The letter is almost without content. It says nothing about his tears. I am thinking, while I write, of The Lesbian Girl.

One day in the darkness of a winter afternoon, he tells me about her. But I already know. I say that she is not really lesbian at all, and that I know how she uses that as a front, to show how she does not need men's love. She is apparently above needing anyone, for anything. She does not love the women who share her bed. She makes love to other women because it is a way of making love to herself. He explains this to me. This is the attraction. I, on the other hand, am so vulnerable that I get sick from loving too much without it being reciprocated. I am horrified by my shaking body.

"Are you attracted to her?"

"I don't know."

"Do you want to sleep with her?"

"No. I don't know."

"Are you in love with her?"

"I told you, I don't know anymore. I can be myself with her."

The words are colder than seventy below. They sink through the soul like hot ice and stick and burn. And then he tells me about how she has gone to Europe, how she will return. There is a dark shadow that has finally obscured me entirely from his view. I see her dark lipstick even though she is in Europe. I feel her coldness. She is not one of the goddesses.

The telephone rings. I pick it up. The American accent. Calling from Europe. The coldness, the hardness, the way she says his name, as if I did not exist in the past or the present, as if I did not also come from Africa.

I give him the receiver. Go to the bathroom. From Europe. She has called him from Europe. He can be himself with her. Perhaps the glass plate is only with me. I faint onto the tiles.

☙

I no longer eat or drink. I no longer mind the bitter cold. I drive the car into a snowbank, and don't look when crossing the slushy intersections. In the cold gray buildings I wait for him sometimes after class. One day I meet her in the lift. The elevator. Going up. I know it is The Lesbian Girl, because of the terror in his eyes. Her hands shake and she says hello, to him. Then she looks at me and tries to smile. Her face is so white it seems blue. She has outlined her lips in black. Her hair falls over her face and she tries to disappear into the background.

After that I see her often. I say to him, ten past two, she'll phone you then. She phones at ten past two. Later, I can predict her steps without effort. This seems to unsettle him.

She has a face like a bird of prey. She is older than I am, and exudes confidence. She is a Lesbian and a Poet, an excellent writer, though unpublished, he says to me.

When you left for America to try and become a writer you did not visualize the intricate repercussions of uprooting yourself. You did not see how your imagination had grown roots in the soil on which you had been standing for twenty-two years. You left your soul behind in the mountains and in the cracks in the pavement outside the Yeoville flat.

The African Literature Guy wears black all the time now. He has rings underneath his eyes.

I grew up under the Apartheid system. For the first few years of school there were very few children who were not white. I learned to speak Afrikaans fluently, because it was the language of the ruling party. You were told very early on that if you failed English or Afrikaans for Matric, you'd have to repeat the whole year. Then bit by bit, black children began to trickle into the school. This was a decade before the official abolition of Influx Control and Apartheid. We played hopscotch in the dusty August sand, and counted the days until the first of Spring which arrived in the form of an electric thunderstorm.

Mama Glynis came to teach us Zulu. She was also a television actress. We never saw her hair since she always wore a brown and blue scarf tightly around her head. We complained about having to learn English Afrikaans, Zulu and German. We were asked which one we'd like taken off the syllabus, except for English and Afrikaans which were compulsory.

So we learned all four languages. The black pupils in the class spoke four or five other languages as well. There was no racial division. I only realize this when I live in the Midwest, and am given the opportunity to view what some call the most segregated city in America.

You learned, being young in Africa that Seeing was not Believing. You watched television when you went to friends because your own family could not afford a TV set, a very expensive and luxurious possession. The news always showed snippets of South African violence, police firing on a dangerous mob, looking vulnerable in their minority, side by side with much more explicit scenes of violence from say, the Middle East.

You'd sit with your friends in the afternoon school break, smelling freshly cut grass, looking at the sharp bright white clouds against blue skies, and they'd say, "but it's terrible everywhere. The whole world is going down the drain. Economies everywhere are sliding. That's just how it is."

"No it isn't," you'd say. "There are things happening here that are unspeakable. There are death-squads, death-camps. The guys who go up to the Angolan border to fight in the army, why do you think they're sworn to secrecy? There's a terrible underground evil that you can feel but not see." And it was true. Later these things were exposed, published, part of the country's common knowledge. But before that, people carried the truth around like a debilitating malady. Your friends of all races reminded you of the vow you'd made never to leave Africa. Years later you shrugged them off in your imagination and told them you'd changed your mind thank you very much.

2

You watched your shadow shorten until in the middle of the day it almost vanished. This was because of the distance from the equator.

2

I write nothing. I wait for some sign from the universe to show me which way to go. There is nothing. I have lost my way entirely. I no longer think of him as The African Literature Guy. I cry for my mother at night.

♫

One day when I was seven years old, I met a man in a park. I was playing on a jungle-gym. He walked by and said hello to me as I hung from a bar and swung my legs.

"Where are your mother and father?"

"There with my brother. That's not my real father, though."

"Aren't you afraid of being this far away from them?"

"Well they can see me and I can see them."

He asked me whether I was a Jew or a Christian. Jew, I said. He was a Christian of sorts. He proceeded to tell me, as I picked an acorn to pieces, that the time was near when the Anti-Christ would incarnate, and we should all, young and old, prepare ourselves for this event. The wind blew through a large oak tree nearby and I was suddenly afraid.

"Where will he come?" I asked.

"To America. He will be born in some strange way, not naturally of course. He will have solutions to the world's social and economic problems. He will be hailed as a hero. All the New Age churches will fall for him. Even the Jews will fall for him. Everything he does will look good but will be evil."

"How will you be able to tell, then?"

"You may not be able to tell. He will be able to read your mind, and so manipulate you."

I think of that man's face from this point in the future, and he himself becomes an Anti-Christ.

My parents had seen the man and started walking back to me. I threw the acorn down at my feet.

"Where's the opposite of America in the world? The exact opposite?"

"Oh, I imagine it's somewhere in the middle of the ocean," he called as he retreated back into nowhere.

The fear he inspired remained with me for years.

⁂

I try to incorporate The Lesbian Girl into the realm of goddesses, but she remains outside. She is cold and hard. If he can be himself with her, I want to love her. It is impossible, eternally set this way. My myth shatters, I see him slipping away from me, from Africa, from the vision of the future we both tried to inscribe in the universe.

⁂

The present days are spent frothing milk. It is in the froth that everything has a chance to emerge. It is in California, that this happens. There is no natural grandeur, no sense of majesty about the setting. Movie-stars cross paths with homeless people. This place is an endless crossing of paths. The surface shimmers with bright lights and brilliant images, but below these, there is a hollowness and once in a while, the earth shudders and threatens to collapse in on itself. I don't mind the superficial smiles of the customers I serve, or the emptiness I feel at the end of the day. Its impact lies in the absence of cold and darkness. The very sameness of the endless, dusty blue days are powerful reminders of darkness and heaviness.

⚘

There is the nightmare of memory. The night in the Gold Toyota. How there are now two women in the world, of different generations, both for whom you will never exist as your true self. Whom you can never meet because parallel lines never converge, even after infinity.

⚘

The day when I drive the car into the snowbank is the coldest day of the year. I drive thinking, this is also his car. I look at his woolen hat, which has frozen to the floor. It is blue, the only colorful thing he wears. He would never have imagined himself wearing a blue woolen hat in the Midwest in America.

I think of the friend who died, how months before, on his twenty-sixth birthday, he remarked that he never thought he'd live that long. A few years before, he was stabbed by an intruder in his house in the middle of the night, and left for dead. He could not believe that he survived such an attack. He thought his life had ended then. And I wonder about him imagining his own death.

When I drive into the snowbank I see the hat on the floor, and it is an unbearable reminder of the love that has nowhere to go.

Far away, in Africa, my family is watching the country change from three hundred years of white rule to black majority rule. I phone them from the cold and hear the sun in their voices. I can hardly speak. They ask if I am all right and I say I am. They want to know how he is, how his studies are going. The conversation moves elliptically around the truth that I'm not able to tell. They tell me about beauty and good will and about shameless violence. My brothers bear witness to atrocities: one day in a traffic jam, a taxi war erupts. A warring taxi faction hauls passengers out of the Toyota minivan and stabs them. No one watching this dares interfere and my family gets home unharmed. Someone we know has been killed. But the drought is over at last, and the most magnificent thunderstorms roll over the sky every afternoon. The garden is like a tropical paradise. The atmosphere of euphoria is tangible. It is like the lifting of a literal curse. The Endless Paradox. The conversation has to end because it's too expensive.

The struggle is with myself: Am I capable of such an enormous projection of my desires onto the world that reality is indistinguishable from these desires?

Or am I unraveling threads that already exist —that have been there for eternity —that make up patterns in the universe and individual lives?

I am entirely obsessed with the environment. It is all gray and old and Germanic. There are hardly any single-storey houses. The buildings crouch on top of one another emitting fumes from leaking gas-pipes. People, I generalize, have been physically distorted by centuries of intermarriage and unbearable winters. It is impossible for the human form to be beautiful under such circumstances. People are like the trees, and blossom only briefly, before they retreat into hardness again after Fall.

The Lesbian Girl lives in an old gray apartment. I know a lot about her. That she has a cat. That the cat has kittens. I know that her toilet is filthy, and that she fancies herself a Witch.

The roads are cracked. The river divides rich from poor, white from black.

Your memory of the place is monochromatic at all times, except for the black and red that pour over the part when you cried for your mother.

As you descend into a vortex of despair, you are always aware of its metaphorical value. You think of Dante's Inferno, even of Alice in Wonderland. You are never alone in this descent, and yet you are alone in your terror.

I have begun to regret that my decision to leave Africa was made out of antipathy.

⚐

One night I get out of bed in the blind agony of her spell. I throw the blankets from me, and the floor creaks under my footsteps. I walk up and down, see the faint blue snow-reflected moonlight through the blinds. I hate her, hate her, I say.

I know he is awake.

I did not think ever that I would see tears, but there they were that time, in the haunted moonlight of a foreign country, from the person who was The African Literature Guy.

The night is a deep black sea and we are adrift, both of us watching a dark cloud of hawks in the rain come toward us, with talons bared —we feel them tear out our organs, we are each other, but there is a plate of glass and I want to smash it open, break it. I wish I had the strength of Hercules; I wish I were a man, or that I was the Lesbian Poet, in love with her own image.

⚐

There is something about a cyclical love-story that is disturbing. The concern is whether because of the absence of so-called linear narrative, there will be any kind of ending. Also, because the author tells the love-story from an obscure point in the journey, there is the risk of an unsatisfactory ending.

Each morning I wake up and remember that I am not myself, that the spell has wrapped itself around me.

When I was at school, I loved the teacher whose high heels clicked down the outside corridor. I sat through lessons, watching the thunderclouds build behind the trees. I looked at the luminous green of the African summer and did not think then that it was the color of my soul. The smell when the rain splattered down onto the hot sand in large heavy drops drifted in through the open window. The teacher would smile, and I wouldn't know then, in the hot beauty of the African day, how the teacher would grow older and how I would see years later, lines burned into her face by too many harsh realities and the absence of love.

⤜

I wish now for the person I was at University, the one who was large enough to experience arrogance. I can't remember being there. Can't remember that once even The African Literature Guy was small and it was I who wished to unbury him.

⤜

I see myself in the old stooped people of another generation. They walk wintry streets, their limbs aching in this uninhabitable climate. They have lost everything. There is no joy in their labored attempts to get to the bus-stop, or the way they buy bread from Pick `n Save.

The boy Jasper who gave me ripe mangoes will never be like these people when he is old. He will never lose the spirit of the mountain to whom he prays every day. He will be in a place which he knows is beautiful and sacred.

I suddenly refuse to see myself in the stooped shadows of an unfamiliar culture. I have begun to walk as they walk, since I already have the inclination to stoop like my real father.

I have not learned the art of flattening out the tapestry of life, so that the picture is even. I cannot escape from the edge.

The images that have been rising to the surface of the steamed milk in California grow more numerous as the days progress. They are so profuse that they begin to assault me. The time in the Midwest, the two years spent there where the days blended into dull copies of one another. Another life of mine on another continent, where, walking down the street you heard the constant bubbling of a foreign and incomprehensible African language, which was like music, and which you realized, in later years, you understood. Your whole life. Trips to the mountains, jumping from forty-foot rocks into cold ink-colored pools. Chasing monkeys away from your doorways in the early hours of the morning. Getting the mail from the mailbox before the snails ate everything. Things you never wrote about. Things you had forgotten.

The assault of these images begins on a day not far from the present, where I work in the café. A customer who is a self-made millionaire asks me on my lunch break where I come from. I tell him it is Africa. He looks at my white apron. At my hair in a childish ponytail, dangling from my head. At my insecure fingers that play with a thread from my apron. He tells me, looking at all this, that I should get an education. One needs an education these days, my dear.

I feel the small shell around myself begin to crack. I straighten up, forget the apron, the thread, the café. I say: I am very educated, my dear.

By this I don't mean any superficial knowledge to which I happen to have access.

I walk away from him breaking, cracking out of the confines of myself, someone caught in the paradox of a specific and difficult location in space and time.

2

In the Midwest, in the clutches of the spell cast by the Lesbian Poet, I begin to see in what tiny mould I have finally been cast.

One day the light outside changes drastically. We sit opposite one another, he and I, trying to outwait the presence of her. We look at the sky. It is darker. The shadows are eerie. I say to him, "this feels like the end of the world." I say, "something is wrong with the sun."

We look out of the windows and see the strange shadows cast by the bony fingers of trees.

The telephone rings.

He picks it up and turns his back to me. I walk to the door, go outside into the cold eerie light of a full solar eclipse.

I hate the ghastly light. When he comes outside, he stands there with his hands in the pockets of his jeans.

"What did she say?"

"She loves it. That the moon blots out the sun. She wants to harness the forces of the moon for a spell."

The sun is a crescent of brilliance outlined by black. The light, which was not that bright to begin with because we are so far north, is obscured by the shape of the moon. The moon itself however is invisible.

Soon, the light begins to brighten. After some minutes it is over. I can't find the moon anywhere in the sky, though I expect to.

We are both self-conscious about the event of an eclipse at this point in the narrative.

I had a dream in Africa once, when I was eleven. In the dream I climbed a tall tree outside our house, but the top was so high that once I had reached it, the roof of the house was a tiny red square far below me. I looked across to another tree where a prince waited for me. Between these two high trees, a thick rope had been strung. He (the prince) beckoned me to walk along the rope to his tree.

Next to me suddenly, stood a witch. She had a hooked nose and a hat and a black tattered gown. She smiled at me reassuringly so that I was confused, not being able to know if she was Good disguised as Evil, or Evil trying to deceive me. Walk the rope, she said, walk it. The prince beckoned again, the witch encouraged me. So I started walking. I looked down, saw the fertile green of our lawn. I looked back at the witch. She took out a large scissors and snipped the rope. As I fell, I caught a glimpse of the prince stretching out his hand. I knew it, I thought, that she'd cut the damned rope. I fell so fast, thought, any second now I'll die, and then landed softly, gently, on the grass beside our house.

*

I sit here in California and look into a mirror in which I see myself sitting in the Midwest, looking back into a mirror of my existence in Africa, where I stare into a mirror of the future. There is no notion of time. Yet years are counted, and by the presence of nostalgia and regret, I understand that I am ever caught up in the illusion of time.

*

I can always recall my mother's face. I can hear her voice. I know her so deeply that I can create her image whenever I like, in my imagination. It is the same with the house. On an afternoon in winter, when he tells me he has gone to her house because she has something to tell him, I have nowhere to go.

So I lie down on the floor of the nondescript apartment. I am immediately flying down the passage in the house, to my mother and stepfather's room at the end. The sunlight is golden on the wooden floor, and the stained glass roundel which my mother made, casts red and purple shadows on the wall. I run my hands over the plaster, feel the solid brick beneath it, bricks, which I had helped carry when we built the house. I reach the arch to the bedroom at the end of the passage. The room is yellow. The arch is hand-sculpted by worn and loving hands, which I look at, as she lies there, my mother, sleeping on the bed. She is barefoot. Her shirt rises and falls as she breathes. Her face is tired. I touch her smooth forehead. Kiss her hands. I look around the room, see the wood of the window-frames, the Egyptian Ibises stalking through the long grass outside. There is a hard glass plate between myself, and this room. I cannot reach in and wake her, and hold her hand tightly and pull her back with me into this other world, where I am trapped as soon as I open my eyes.

&

When he comes back from the apartment with the cat that has kittens and the dirty toilet seat, I can smell her perfume on his shirt. It is a clinging suffocating smell. I can barely be in the same room with him. He says that he hugged her. That she cried and told him she loved him, that there was no one else for her. No single soul in this entire world whom she could love as she loved him. The Lesbian Girl said this.

If every artistic creation of mine, and every book and vision and dream and struggle of mine had physical dimension, I would be the queen of a huge empire.

This is impossible to contain in a dark winter coat that weighs ten pounds. It is also unimaginable how it all lies compressed beneath a small white apron in a seaside café.

I am unable to stop smelling the perfume, as if she lingers all around me at all times. I start to see her name, in car license plates, road names, restaurants. She is as inescapable as the place.

For the first time it is clear to me that I am faced with a reality more ugly than the one I thought to escape. The racial segregation in this Midwestern city is extreme, to the point that I have not spoken once to a person of another race or country. I am aware that the stereotype of a racially divided society in South Africa, which clashes with the reality of the actual tangled integration, is the perfect scapegoat for the stereotype of a free America, and the reality of its harsh, silent racism.

I am tired of the farce, the dull facade, the image, the appearance, the smoothing over, the spell, the distance from the truth, the glass plate between ourselves.

I receive no reply from The Journalist, after the single letter. I imagine he is angry with me for writing, I begin to believe I wrote out of selfish desperation to regain something that was lost, to remind myself of who I was. I hoped, perhaps, for a reply which would give this to me.

I want to burn down the city and its old tired sulking buildings, and tear up the pavements. I want to smash in every single Winter Box noisily housing people, recycling air and water and other putrid substances. My hands tremble with the desire to break, to crack, to annihilate everything, telephone and electricity cables; I want to be a giant and stalk the oppressive streets, squashing people with small minds who have crushed me, tearing out the church bells that toll mournfully from pseudo-European churches. They ring a particularly hypocritical note.

⌇

There is not much money but there is enough, and in America these things are more easily done than ever in Africa. I book a ticket home. Home, Africa. My mother. I have to go back though perhaps not to stay, and to be far enough away from him.

I say goodbye to him at the bus-stop. It is a cold hollow evening. We hug each other, and my heart is breaking, because it contains a love too great perhaps, for what is possible.

I fly from winter, into the night, across Greenland, Iceland to Europe. I sit in silence, not sleeping, or eating.

The plane lands in London. I take the tube from Heathrow to Covent Garden. The grass is still green even though it is winter. There are people everywhere, new films have come out that I haven't seen. Things are happening in the world and I have no knowledge of them. Suddenly everything is coherent. People are reading books. Conversations that I overhear are about politics, theories of discourse and the artistic genius of William Blake, now on exhibition at the Tate Gallery.

In the afternoon I go back on the tube to the airport, and catch the night flight to South Africa.

I fly over the Mediterranean. The sky is dark, but the stars are near and clear. The moon is below me. The face in the moon is hard to see.

Dawn comes very early. I have forgotten. Below me I see white clouds, and beneath that, the rich red earth of the African continent. It is as though my soul rushes down and merges with the land. I feel attached to it as we fly over it. My heart beats furiously. I wish he were with me.

The sunrise is a symphony of color. The sea of clouds breaks open and allows fiery rays across the world. My eyes burn; I can barely let in such brilliance.

I am pale and fluid as the reflection of the moon in water when I arrive. I am back home, in Africa. My brothers are tall young men. They are brown and healthy. The first thing they say prods me to become uncomfortably self-aware.

"You're so small."

They seem happy. My mother's arms are softer around me than in my dreams.

We go back from the airport to the house, the house that I have haunted in my dreams for so long. The grass is green and the ochre walls are more solid, larger than in the imagination. There is a thundercloud above the house as we go into the drive and my heart is in the cloud and will break simultaneously.

There is the clatter of raindrops on the iron roof, the smell of wet earth, of fertility. I am the outsider, the intruder into a once-connected circle. They make way for me as if I have never been away. As if The African Literature Guy did not exist.

We drink tea to the sound of the rain. The drops outside are warm.

I see that the chairs in the lounge have aged. The cane furniture from the time I was with The Journalist creaks louder than it used to. The house looks more rustic than in my imagination. The ceiling leaks water next to the plastic skylight, and the drops make a loud ringing sound as they land in a metal bucket. My mother is strong. I am blown by the breeze through the open window —a feather shaking in the warm outbreath of my younger siblings. It all converges like rushing rivers over a cataract; I am back where I started, where we started and he is there —a thousand light-years away, the eclipse of the sun and The Lesbian Girl. I am caught in a time warp, and have not come full circle.

I am back in the same garden where I last saw The Journalist. I think briefly of my letter to him.

The brothers play music. I have forgotten about music.

They want to know about America, and I am unable to speak.

My old bedroom seems to contain no memory of my past.

I sleep through the night deeper than I have slept in years. Old nightmares return, robbers come up the drive. An army of militant warriors surround the house and it is the end. But I wake to the sound of birds and throw open the windows to the magic of a cleanly washed shining African day. Both are real.

*

At this point it could be that I am an exile returning home after the inauguration of the first black president in South Africa.

*

The person who walks out into the garden is shrunken and pale. She hides from the brilliance and the color. She has forgotten how the warmth of the sun has the potential to seep through everything and melt anguish. She has been so divided, so fragmented, that she no longer remembers properly what the factors were that made her a cohesive whole in this world.

I lie in the grass and dig my fingers into the earth. It is warm, pulsating at the same rate as my heart. I have dreamt of this for so long, but not that I would be here without him.

The Ibises are there, walking through the long grass. They are regal birds.

It is on this first day back in Africa that I go to see the teacher whose heels clicked down the school corridors. She lives where she used to live. Her garden is purple with the sprinkle of jacaranda blossoms. Her face is lined, and she tells me, as we sit on her verandah and look out over rolling hills and savanna, that marriages were certainly not made in heaven. She tells me that her husband is, of course, a millionaire. That she married for love, and lost it, and now devotes her life to the children who sleep in the doorways of shops and who scavenge through garbage cans before dawn. She says the fact that he is a millionaire means she can do as she pleases. She has grown small, but she is still beautiful, and I am able to tell her then, that I love her.

The telephone rings late at night, and from where I sleep on a mattress on the floor, I can reach it. The window is open and the sound of crickets pulses through the night. I hold the cold receiver to my ear.

His voice.

How am I?

I'm happy to be with everyone at last.

It's ten below zero. But he's working hard. He doesn't mind the cold so much.

I miss him terribly. I can barely say so.
He misses me too.

Silence of snow. Noise of the crickets. The cold morning of
the Midwest and the warm evening of South Africa.

He dreamt that I was his sister and woke up feeling better.
I am not a sister. This, here, in Africa, is where *my* brothers
are.
He's not sure of anything anymore. He just has to work. He
says he will phone again on the weekend.

There is nothing else. I put down the phone. The silence
is the silence that surrounded us when we used to make love
—the absence of words that annihilates.

The green giants which are trees bend over the house and
shower the lawn with tiny white blossoms. You walk with damp
feet over the morning dew and clusters of blossoms cling to
your toes and stick to your heels. You see, in the way the breeze
sways the branches, the echoes of goddesses, of something you
have lost, of a gesture, a flick of the wrist which is no longer
yours. Your desires have dissipated and are invisible even to
yourself.

I climb up hills with my brothers and my legs are scratched by thorns and rocks. I watch sunsets. The fast descent of the sun is because we are in the southern hemisphere. Twilight lasts for a few minutes, and then it grows dark and we follow one another's blue shadows even though we are older.

They don't ask about him.

There is the love affair with the land, and with the self that I meet back in Africa. I am euphoric and heartbroken as I lie beneath the leaves of a jasmine bush and watch the white billowing clouds rush over me. I let myself sleep on the wet green earth in the country of my birth.

I follow the pull of Cape Point, travel two thousand kilometers in an old car to the edge of the world. I stand at Cape Point on a clear hot day, buffeted by the wind, hair spiraling upward in whirls of salt and sea-spray. The colors are vivid, bluer and clearer than hallucinations. It smells as if a huge spirit resides here. If I have nothing, I have this place. I have the love for this blue deep Indian-meeting-Atlantic Ocean. The place exists in books, in dreams dreamt whilst in the cold bitter winter of Wisconsin. In the past, the present, and in the future as I look back.

I see the whole mass of humanity, their insanity as they rush around the surface of the earth, between machines and electric wires, whole lives buzzing with a frequency intolerably high —I see what it is, living in America, in boxes, made of paper heated by wires —complex, absurd. I try to relinquish my secret desire to have money.

I reel and falter at the edge of the world, find nothing in the structure of the Invisible that can support me. I fall off the wire I have been walking along for so long.

I think of him at night when the South-Easter howls down the herb-covered, crystal-infested mountain. I watch the moon rise over the sea. It has a different face. I hear singing from a church in the wooded valley. The voices cut through me.

I am in Cape Town, and it is almost three years since I left Africa.

It is at this point that I see The Journalist again. He steps out of his new car and hitches his trousers. I find him, his voice, his face, unchanged. The broken smile still hovers around his face. The day is windy and he stands next to his car, his hair blown forward, white.

His love has not changed.

We walk in a forest, the pine needles catch our shoes and socks. He finds it hard to believe that I am walking next to him. My eyes are dry and his are wet. And he is angry.
And I am lost.
He says an injured man died in his arms after he'd been shot in the townships the day before. The reason for his tears.

I try to explain, what it was, when I left —how I interlock with him, The African Literature Guy, how we blindly follow an impulse across the world, South Africa-London-America to find ourselves in a vindictive dismal town.

The Journalist wets my shoulder with his tears.

The prison in this pine forest is inescapable. I have no way out. I cannot touch the sad face, listen to the sound of his heart. There is just a moment, frozen somewhere; the night in the gold Toyota that exists somewhere between dreams.

And then he says that I should know, how afterwards he went back to her, how she, as a good friend, gave him comfort. How he went to others for the same reason, to try to find what was gone. How he could not recapture it, and wanders through ancient musty mazes of bookshelves in his dreams, and finds nothing but his own charred bones in a heap in some old cellar.

I tell him about waking up in the middle of the night in a place thousands of miles away from home, of finding the advert for SUBS on the fridge, of going back to bed, of that madness.
The goddess begins to form again, against all odds as his eyes rest on the curve of my shirt, the long hair over my shoulders, the turn of a wrist which he once held in his hand.
When he asks me whether I am still in love, I say it is the same. That I love The African Literature Guy, who is in America.

And when I say goodbye to him, the hole in the universe rushes in and closes itself quickly and in our human state we are as powerless as trees moved by the wind.

I think of him in the Midwest where you can't drink the water or breathe the air. Everything that is destructive is hidden and invisible. Like she is —The Lesbian Girl, who appears by some obtuse reversal of fortune, confirming the fear of the past as if it were already written in the stars and there was no freedom to change it.

The African Literature Guy does not phone again on the weekend. Some weeks later, he tells me over the phone that he will be in Africa —in Zimbabwe.

We have no more money in the account. He uses the last money for his flight.

I know from where I stand in the future, that she took him to the airport. It was bitterly cold and she drove him the two hour journey, and sat with him there, holding his hand in her icy one. She said goodbye to him, kissed him, said that she wished she were coming with him to Africa. She held him tightly in her heart as if I did not exist.

He thought of her on the plane, through the long night as he followed the path over Greenland and Iceland and Europe. The shortest distance across the world is a curve. On a flat map, it seems an insane journey to travel from America to the Arctic Circle, on the way to the southern hemisphere. He flew across the Mediterranean to the African continent, and carried her American accent with him through the clouds.

The story circles in on itself, as if it has lost its way. The narrative in its innocence becomes an unraveling of clichés. The reader wonders at having to work so hard. Perhaps the reader enjoys working hard. Or perhaps nothing more than honesty is required from the reader, and working hard has nothing to do with it.

The reader is embraced as part of everything.

I have found therefore, a single way in which it is possible to be rendered visible.

I walk through mountains where only baboons and Boomslang can be found, and where the nearest form of civilization is a farmer's stone house at the edge of a gorge. I listen to the sounds of the people as they talk, and I understand the words they use. The language is not just a bubbling waterfall of foreign sounds.

I see a car stolen before me in the streets of Cape Town.

I see men with rocks chasing a young boy and I am almost sick to death.

I know what they do.

I know that in this harsh continent there is very little mercy.

It could be that my real self will never surface and waves of time will wash over all the painful attempts at definition.

What does the universe think of such a possibility?

The universe is not conscious of clichés. The word 'cliché' is imposed on a wider, deeper, profounder recurring pattern. The universe finds itself colonized and flattened small to fit into the narrowness of a word.

In Zimbabwe there is a bottomless pool.

In a cave. As blue as space.

The bottom has never been discovered and the reason for the color is a mystery. Sunlight pours down through a circular opening, lighting the pool.

I stand there with The African Literature Guy. He is shadowy, from a light-deprived existence in North America. He smells different, as if her spell lingers on his shirt, in the buttonholes of his shirt. Her perfume, or her spell. I am dizzy, not thinking about the blue or the depth, or the wild green plants that cling to the faces of ancient rock. There are passages in this system of caves that are now called Chinoyi, which one might follow into the heart of the earth. I wish to hide myself in one of the dark tunnels, to escape the cracking of my heart as I wait for him to speak.

❧

I slip away from myself. There is just a female form, her shadow large against the granite intrusions. He has his hands in his pockets, and then after a while, takes one out, touches her face. She wants to move but she seems to be frozen, paralyzed. She fears herself very much. Her voice, her movements. He shapes her hair around her face, looks at her closely, as if trying to decide.

A rainbird calls from the white-thorned tree known as the acacia. Its notes sink down into the ground.

They stand there without moving as a smooth brown snake glides over the floor of the cave. Its back catches rays of sun and then it vanishes into the shadows.

He looks at her for the first time. She knows it is the first time. She does not know what to do with herself, or where to look. She wants to scrape the foreign smell from him and drown it in the deepest blue.

The images are images of insanity and schizophrenia, but they are held within the frame of a narrative.

Clothes fall from her like old rose petals plucked by the breeze. Only she is followed by The Lesbian Girl.
She wishes to know whether he ever made love to The Lesbian Girl. Or only contemplated it —imagined it.

It makes her ill, nonetheless. There may be more words that pass between them, but she is never sure. Even in the future, looking back into the cave, she is never quite sure.

And then they make love in the cave, on the damp floor over which a snake has recently slithered. There is an ancient smell as if air, or secrets trapped within the cave passages are suddenly released, after having been caught there for thousands of years.

Across the wide silences of Zimbabwe as we travel toward Domboshawa, I am aware of the absence of resonant American accents which have the attention-getting quality of general public announcements. Time may indeed be dismissed in this realm of ticking bugs in the late afternoon. The sky is made of the heaviest crystalline blue, and it folds itself around the hills, around the women and children who walk along the roadsides clothed only in blankets.

It is heavy like this because somewhere you dared not believe that you would make love to him again.

⟁

If the narrative wanted to be consistent with certain feminist canons, it would have made certain that the narrator asserted herself without the presence of The African Literature Guy. It would have dismissed him now from the text.

⟁

Domboshawa is sunk in mists. The huge granite expanse is pink and purple through the low cloud. You walk up through the whispering grass in silence. You can hear the echoes of the secrets of the world as you walk. You hear the harsh voice of The Lesbian Girl, the crunch of her boots on snow. You can see her tears run streams of black mascara down her face.

You hear her telling him in the dirty apartment, that he is the only one to whom she can connect. You feel yourself growing large with anger as you climb the rock. You are not sure whether mist or tears moisten your face. You need to blow your nose. The wind, at that moment, in its generosity, carries you a tissue from nowhere. You say:

"You see, I can also use magic when necessary."

He stops and your eyes meet. You feel like a child, see yourself as the same person who lived in Africa as a child. The clothes you wear now are no different from those you wore when nine years old. You have the same kind of jeans and shirt. Your hair is long and falls over your face when you bend to tie your shoelace. You are uncomfortably bigger inside than out. And then without warning you punch The African Literature Guy hard on his shoulder, and he stumbles and falls back onto the rock. You realize then that you are crying, as he catches your wrist, and tries to hold you to himself saying: "What are you doing? What are you doing?"

I am pulled back to the place, and the moment at Domboshawa from the edge of the American continent where I work in a café all day long. It happens one night.

After The Lesbian girl, after the Midwest and the terrible winters, after the first return to Africa.

I am in this place in California writing about The Lesbian Girl, and a letter arrives in the mail. There is no return address. And without anything more, I know it is from her. I sense her so strongly. I know that she is aware of me because I have been writing about her.

So I sleep, and in the night, through my dreams, I see an icy hand reaching for my heart. It finds it, and clamps bitterly cold fingers around it, squeezing it, so that I wake up. The icy grip continues, and pulls my soul back to Domboshawa, to the Chinoyi Caves, to Africa.

Here in America, I hover between being and non-being. I am no longer in a cold place. I thought it was merely the cold that destroyed the spirit. But it is more than that. When I scratch away at the shiny surface, the underneath caves in and it is quite hollow. I think, no wonder they have earthquakes. I am afraid of seeing a pattern repeated, and wish immediately to apologize to the universe for carrying a bitter taste in my mouth when people ask me: How many of you English are down there in Africa?

I feel African but have white skin. This is mostly problematic out of Africa. Or in the realm of extreme self-consciousness.

Through the mist over Domboshawa, he followed you as you ran down the rock. You could hear him breathing hard, could hear the echoes of cattle lowing miles and miles away. The acoustics were deceptive in this place. You passed a goatherd driving his goats up a remote part of the rock, and he greeted you both in Shona as you ran by.

"Wait," The African Literature Guy called. "Wait!"

But you didn't. You heard the wind in your ears, felt the smatter of drops against your cheeks, and the chattering echoes of footstep after footstep down the steep slopes of the giant brown granite rocks.

As you ran almost perpendicular to the ground, you thought of the dam wall you climbed somewhere on some farm when you were ten or so, how your footsteps echoed strangely across the floor of the empty reservoir. How between the cracks and weeds on the floor you found the tiny bones of a mouse, and tried to put them together in the shape of a human skeleton. You thought of it as beautiful. You were upset that you had the rib-cage, the legs and arms and yet no skull. You were later told that the thing you carried preciously between the folds of tissue paper came from an unhygienic mouse skeleton and had to be left where it was found.

You were the same person as you ran through the whispering grass away from The African Literature Guy.

In the grass you found an old reservoir, not unlike the one with the mouse bones. You climbed into it, and leaned against the wall, your blood pounding violently in your temples.

He reached you at last.

It is possible to intervene with the flow of time and to reverse the passage of events by changing direction. To turn from him meant that the spiral that had been whirling inward could do so no more.

The air was thick with the smell of plants. We had our backs against the old walls of the water reservoir. I told him that I had seen The Journalist. He said: "While you were here, I behaved as if I was on my own." He said he knew there were consequences of doing that, and took my limp cold hand.

"You've torn a huge hole in the mythology which is my life." I said and my nose ran like ink from an unreliable pen.

I had shrunk to the smallest size. Compressed until the gravity was so dense that I would suck in everything, the world, the stars, the moon, space, time and The African Literature Guy. White Giant Blue Dwarf Black Hole —an implosion, which would result in the birth of a new galaxy with its own planetary system as the spiral inward began to undo itself.

It is true, that no matter which hemisphere you are in, no matter which way up the moon is, its face is invariably sad. In the northern hemisphere, it appears that tears have carved into the moon's left eye, gouged furrows down the left hand side of its face. In the southern regions, the moon's right eye weeps, tears seem to have been blown up over the forehead by some cosmic wind and the traces can never be wiped from the surface, because they are not surface tears.

I am blocked by my own passion. It is too large to find expression in anything artistic. The African Literature Guy cannot bear such a force. I find a moment of release when I think of watching my mother sleep, of watching the face that I have loved for twenty-four years. Of knowing that she does not sleep on her bed only in a dream I have of her while I am in Wisconsin, but literally as I watch her. I think of her while in Zimbabwe, while trying to understand why it is that The Lesbian Girl reduces me to nothing and is able to eclipse me.

The velvet night skies over Africa are punctured with large thick metallic stars. They shine down through the haze and glitter of the Milky Way, and dissolve time and the small struggles of human beings. I am with The African Literature Guy in Zimbabwe at the top of World's View. The rocks are illuminated by the setting moon. The drop from the edge of the precipice is so great that you could fall for ages before hitting the bottom. During the day you can look out over a distance of hills and knolls reaching a three hundred kilometer radius.

"I'm going back to America," he says through the wind. "To finish the Doctorate."

"I know."

"What do you want to do?"

The call of an owl, the rustle of the wind through grass and boulders. He folds his arms as the wind catches his hair and blows it forward over his face. He is sad because it is so long since he was able to play music. The musician's hands drop to his sides and wring my heart with their emptiness. We face one another.

He says, "it's not the end."

The mud huts in Africa that dot the slopes of hills and nestle in wide green valleys are more private and beautiful than the cardboard luxury condominiums of North America. Grass and trees and sand open out in front of each hut. Nature is the garden. I remember Jasper who gave us mangoes, who loved his life, who felt blessed to walk this rich red earth. I am humbled by the force of all my illusions, as they crumble. I think of my mother telling me not to leave out of antipathy.

Now, as I prepare to leave Africa once more, I have no desire to go. I see the same pattern repeat itself. I must undo it. I have no home. Or perhaps the hollow center of my being, through which I fall at night like a child falling off its bed, has more to do with The African Literature Guy.

Before I leave Africa again, I take in great gasps of the blue sky, I wish to scrape the scent of wood from the windowsills and keep it in a bottle. I want to pack jacaranda blossoms in my suitcase until it is filled to bursting. I want to carry back with me, sand, mud, crystals from the mountains; I wish to find Jasper and my past, and bring everything with me. I wish for the power to undo the great knot in the universe that exists because of a day, a minute, a second, in a gold Toyota in the waving winter grass.

I have to say goodbye to my mother, to my family. I leave Africa again, to go back to America with The African Literature Guy.

*

I thought America was where people went who wanted to become writers. I did not understand the first time what that would mean.

*

It is possible that I am one of a handful of rootless Africans —from Ghana, Nigeria, South Africa, white, black— writing to fill the void of uprooting, to stay the tide of insanity, to create a world separate from the one where you go to work every day in a city where smog and violence and technology cause as much destruction of the human spirit as you feared would happen through the wars in Africa. Only here in America it is more invisible. And there is no more beauty. I begin to believe that society here no longer progresses. It has begun to destroy itself, collapse in on itself. There is just the endless destruction of the environment, the desperate attempts at undoing what harm has already been done. But it is the human suffering in Africa that breaks me, and I allow it to.

꒰

It is in this frame of mind that I come back into the bitter cold of winter, feel the rush of an arctic wind against my skin, as the gray solid derelict buildings of the Midwestern city appear through the fog on the bus window.

꒰

I think about the existence of black holes in space, can barely grasp the concept as I struggle to make the jump into a non-rational way of perception. This is my battle as I walk harshly through the wind to the department where The African Literature Guy is finishing his Doctorate. The existence of black holes. The magnetism. Why it is that if it's "out there" we are prepared to acknowledge the existence of something beyond our absolute understanding, and here on earth we look quite desperately for a rational explanation to every occurrence. Take the existence of cancer. Of violence. Take, for example, the fact of The Lesbian Girl. Perhaps something with the magnetic force of a black hole is exerting its power over me. I am being pulled, sucked into a vacuous nothing, a deep void of non-existence.

What chance do I have of resisting? I lecture myself this way until I have made it through the cold. Once in the gray dull warmth of the building, I look up.

She is standing there, her hair over her eyes. She has been to Europe and back. Wearing black. All the time. She has dyed her hair, I think. Her hands shake, and her eyes retreat. She looks small, but she is larger than I feel. She clutches a book about the Cosmos between her shaking blue-white hands.

She knows who I am.

I see that she is also going to see him, to give him the book. I smell her perfume. I have just arrived back from Africa. The curve of her face is set in the direction of The African Literature Guy. I begin to break, to move outwards, away from the shadow. Before I rupture into a million shards of unidentifiable Nothing, I must get out of the building. Out of the shadow, the huge heavy darkness. It is then that I turn violently from her, go back out into the cold where my heart beats white heat through my veins.

ᴥ

It is easy to make airline reservations in America. If you have your own computer, and an internet connection, you can do it yourself. I have the room inside myself to appreciate this fact as I think of Africa, of the enormous expenses there, of the difficulties of living there. I try to focus on this, not on the beauty, or the magic, or that Jasper loved the mountainside in Nyanga, Zimbabwe, near the border of Mozambique.

I know people in California, and so I phone them and cry as I ask them for a favor. It would be no problem for them if I wanted to go there. They would be happy to help someone in need, by offering them a job immediately in their café next to the beach. The person who receives this offer says thank you, and throws blindly, some shorts and scarves into a bag, thinking of the sun, of the warmth, of the undoing of a spiral.

The flight is inexpensive. The people in California pay for it with their credit card, telling their young friend that she can repay them when she has the money.

The same day that she encountered The Lesbian Girl, she was on a plane to California, having hardly been back in the Midwest.

The light filters through golden sunset smog. Palm trees are outlined along the beach. Fishermen stand tranquilly on the pier. My apartment is tiny and expensive and dark and downstairs. The ocean is four blocks away. I work as much as I can, for five dollars an hour. I froth milk for cappuccinos. I wake up when it is dark and go in before six to slice the meat for sandwiches. I am silent inside my head. I marvel at the absence of words, at how much has taken place without them. I wonder if this silence is the curse I brought down on my life, when I refused to listen to a voice of heartbreak which said to me a long time ago: one day this will happen to you.

I think, perhaps, that I will never write again. I think that he knows where I am, that they, the friends, thought it their duty to write to him and tell him that I was living in California.

$$\mathcal{Q}$$

They don't know that I write, or that I ran to escape the eclipse. They find me strange, the people who work in the café with me. I find myself strange. These hands, this face, this white uniform is not mine. *They* are the other workers. They are ten or so years younger than I am, but they think I am one of them. I am shocked when I look in the mirror, and see such a young face. I feel ancient. I begin to take a liking to my disguise.

$$\mathcal{Q}$$

I dream of tidal waves. Night after night I am running as fast as I can as the water rises. I am with a group. There is an evacuation team helping people escape the mounting tide. I run from the group because I have no trust in their methods. I go off on my own, climbing higher and higher, up mountains and more mountains. At the top I find that there are people following me. They want to rest but I say, as long as this wave keeps mounting we can't stop. They agree with me and soon I am the leader of the evacuees, but I feel strong even as I contemplate the possibility of death. As soon as I no longer fear dying, the water begins to subside.

His absence is at times so unbearable that I think of jumping off the pier. I know though, that I would swim with all my might until I reached the shore.

I believe that this is in fact the end, and that he was mistaken when he said it was not.

I meet a customer who is a white, Afrikaans South African. He is very polite. He tells me that before he was saved and came to America, he worked for the South African Secret Police in the Special Forces. I know that under Apartheid, such men were responsible for eliminating civilians who posed a threat to the white government. I think of the black journalist who was shot outside his home just before Apartheid ended.

One day, I am just closing the door of my apartment to go down to the sea. I hear someone say my name.

My name.

I drop the keys.

I know him but I have never seen him before. Not like this. Perhaps like this in dreams or visions which I have long since stopped having. The African Literature Guy calls me by my name. Over his shoulder is a bag that I have forgotten about, that comes from Zimbabwe. He seems to smell faintly of the African sun. He doesn't look the same as the distant stranger who came back to Africa. He can hear my heart.

I hug him and his body is hot. His face is in my hair. He drops the bag. He says my name.

I am aware that it will not be long and I will be right in the present, having relinquished the advantage of existing in the future of a narrative. I know that it will be possible for me then to lose this perspective.

He comes into my apartment. It reminds me suddenly of the Yeoville flat, where I visited him and lost my soul.

I have hardly any furniture. A mattress on the floor. Some cups, a plate. A board on a suitcase for a table. His eyes rest on the tiny things, the grocery list crumpled up next to the telephone. On the wall there is an old photograph of the two of us in Africa. He takes it down and keeps his eyes on it.

"I came to tell you," he says as tears close his throat. "That I miss you so much. That I love you."

I start to cry. He kisses my mouth, sets the picture down.

"Have I lost you?" The African Literature Guy speaking. The one in his arms is the same person who came to visit him in the Yeoville flat. I am frightened and begin to shake.

"Have I?"

I try to speak, but there are no words.

He tightens his arms. "The spell is broken."

"What did you do?"

"I told her that I loved you."

I think of the apartment, of the cat that is black, of the kittens and an eclipse of the sun.

"When I found out you'd left that day, we went for a walk into the forest. It was cold, but the sun was shining. In the light I suddenly couldn't understand how I'd come to be walking there, with her, in that forest, wearing the clothes I was wearing." He says he never wants to go back to the Midwest.

Silence.

"I felt your absence terribly."

My eyes are on his face, the tautness of lips that were once soft. His voice is uneven. He tells me it had to do with him, with what he thought he didn't have himself. He says that he is his own dead moth—that both the moths in his old nightmare are his, and have nothing to do with me.

I think that possibly beneath her black clothes and boots and the mascara there is someone who was just a girl once.

The African Literature Guy puts his hand on my heart.

2

Two people walk away from the closed door of the apartment. They walk the four blocks to the sea. Over the ocean, the sun is a red giant, hovering behind the oil-rigs and a large steamer. He is tired and his eyes are lined. He has not slept.

It's like it is in books, he says. He doesn't let me go. His hand clasps mine and both palms sweat. I speak of a book.
He wants to see it but it doesn't exist, I tell him.

He understands. That I have lost trust, and yet have not. That I am shrunken and yet cannot be crushed. His eyes sting. He is not thinking, this time, of the Lesbian Girl.
He says, "I'm sorry for all this pain."

It's exactly as it happens in books. The girl, who knew that if she threw herself into the sea, she would try not to let herself drown, is embraced by The African Literature Guy.
He'll do his thesis from California, he says, "if I haven't lost you."
"You haven't lost me," I say.
We are two characters in a single story. In our dreams, we walk down a dirt road. The landscape around us is always changing, but the road is an African road. Our feet are bare and can feel the earth. Behind us, thunder rumbles.

The next day I wake up and look at the warm dent in the pillow next to mine. I hear water boiling on the stove.

He comes into the room carrying tea. I can't see where to hold the cup because of tears. The tea tastes salty.

It is around this time, very close to the present, that the images begin to appear in the froth of the milk I steam for the cappuccinos. I still work in the early mornings, and in the afternoons, when I come home, he is there. Always, he is there with the energy of a lover.

In the afternoon we draw the blinds and sink down onto the sheets. Arms hard, arms soft, hands that revealed the depth of their owner, so that it was possible to slip into a deep abyss and risk never crawling out, carry me passionately to the end of the day. And the silence breaks.

I am not untouched. Uninjured. A narrative begins —every day as I pour the milk into the small tin jug before steaming it, the next episode emerges.

And so it is here, where the glass plate has dissolved entirely, that I begin to write. We begin to laugh, at everything. We begin to love things, shells on the beach, the tiny white poodles belonging to old ladies. We laugh and love things at the same time. As I write and think about The Lesbian Girl, and feel quite certain that she is somehow present, she too is busy writing. Perhaps at the very same hour at which I first recall the spell into the narrative, she puts a letter, his name and address typed neatly on the front, into a mailbox in the cold autumn of another year in the Midwest.

And when the letter arrives, after I return from work, a little further on in the narrative, without looking at it, I tell him: from her.

"How do you know?"

"Smell it."

The moon is full. It is magnified on the horizon through the smog, to surrealistic proportions.

As I walk along the pier I wonder how these millions and millions of people can all possibly be individuals, with lives and dreams and destinies interconnecting, disconnecting. It feels as though there are too many, as though some are perhaps deprived of a self at the expense of someone else. Matter sucked into the hungry void of a black hole.

I dip back from the beach in California, and try to uncover the layers of history and mythology that surround the continent of my birth. I am woven into one of these layers, a single soul amidst so many, finding myself in a particular time, a particular place. Born a certain color, into a certain life.

I look back now at this place with a love that wishes to forgive everything.

Civilizations have come and gone. Over the ancient holy sites of long-forgotten tribes in Africa, other tribes built their own temples, which in turn fell to ruin. Invaders, colonizers, archaeologists, historians, all of them have left marks, have tried in their own way to unravel the tangle in which they find themselves because of the notion of Time. Have tried to place themselves and the world in an order. The tendency toward sequences, lines, consequences, when the universe itself did not ask to be defined.

In South Africa, which I left because I wanted to be free of political and ideological constraints, there is now a new irony, a new cliché: because White Rule is officially over, writers allied with the previous cause, the previous struggle, face their own demise. It is no longer considered appropriate for writers to refer to social or political contexts. Those themes are old and must be forgotten. There is a new prescription, a glass wall of a different nature: the past must be eliminated from present consciousness. Those who prescribe will timelessly take on the task of Rewriting History, continually, layers upon layers, compelled to try and wipe the slate clean, recreate reality so that they may be comfortable, for the moment.

The African Literature Guy brushes the letter and its contents aside. The thread that The Lesbian Girl sends out, like a gossamer spider's web, does not catch. I feel it dangling there loosely, her desire, her ache. I watch the waves tumbling over themselves, thankful for the expanse of ocean, a space over which my soul can race. He leaves it there hanging, her thread. I can feel him leaving it there, walking away from it. I can see it, I almost haven't the strength myself to look away from it.

Eventually, the thread will become thin. Somewhere in the middle it will break, and shrink back into itself.

I lie awake at night. I can hear the noise of the world, as if every television set, radio, every conversation and argument had found its way into my head. His face is soft in sleep, but he seems disturbed. He turns over.

It was perhaps, simply the desire for material comfort that attracted me to America. What was it that made me lose the fear that I had had as a child, the fear that made me want to live as far as possible on the face of the earth from America?

It was the later thought about America, the later impulse —to become a writer, whatever that meant then, that dissolved the fear, and the memory of the fear.

He wakes up and touches my hand.

"Is there really such a noise, or is it in my head?" I ask him.

"They're really making a racket out there."

"Feels like there's no silence in the whole country."

"But think. You can have two television sets, two cars, ten radios, printers and computers..."

"It isn't important to me anymore." I say.

"Why not?"

"I miss the racket of crickets in the jungle and squawking birds that wake me at five."

"But when your car breaks down it takes five months to fix."

"I know. And your washing, which you do by hand, gets stolen off the line because others need it more than you do."

"And a load of shopping costs the equivalent of what the average person there earns in a year."

"Well, we don't have any way of earning money back there anyway."

"That's why we came here."

"I don't know. We came here to almost lose each other."

"Let's go for a walk."

"Now? It's so late."

"Why not?"

The moon hangs over the pacific and the waves throw themselves against the pier. We walk to the edge. We are tired, and stand holding hands, looking out over water that wraps itself round the world. In California, I tell him, it is the absence of cold that helps the most, not the presence of something large and meaningful. The canopy of night stretches over us, and the stars reflect and break in the waters below. Beyond their lives, some stars only live as light.

From this vantage point, Orion is inside out and his belt hangs the wrong way around his waist. In the southern hemisphere, he exists as a mirror image. I see Time stretching out behind me and ahead of me, and it no longer holds to the sequences I've imposed on it. It becomes a landscape through which we travel.

We are here looking out across the Pacific some time after midnight, characters in our own story, mirror images of ourselves that we recognize in the wide silences of Zimbabwe, or in the wind at Cape Point.

Somewhere far in the future, I see that these same characters have grown old. They are still holding hands, moving through the terrain that connects them.

We walk back to the apartment through the wind.

For the first time in your life, you no longer want to rescue your family —not even your father, not the younger brothers who are tall and beautiful beneath the strong African sun.

You think of the mother whose hands are soft, who does not do anything out of antipathy, of how each day after her work she may rest in the silence of an afternoon, the light golden through the windows, the sound of birds louder than human voices. She can wake up and brush her hair and listen to the distant rumble of thunder. You think of the garden at home, of how once a man from Mozambique taught you how to garden, how to plant tomatoes and beans according to the cycles of the moon, of how for two consecutive years the family had armsful of giant red tomatoes and long string beans.

You hold the threads that tangle you, even this far across the world with the people you love, and you no longer pull them towards you.

You think of the brothers who said: "you're so small," as if the picture they had of you before was much larger than the person you had become.

The African Literature Guy has almost finished his doctorate. After all this time, dreams of an old war wake him at night. He begins to unearth the remnants of a lost self.

The African Literature Guy begins to play music again.

The image of frothing milk for cappuccinos loses significance. It was one point of departure.

About the Author

Shelley Davidow is originally from South Africa. She has lived and worked in South Africa, Zimbabwe, England, Germany, Qatar and the United States, among many things as a waitress, researcher, teacher, lecturer and mother, more or less in that order.

In the Shadow of Inyangani (young adult novel), was nominated for the first African Writer's Prize by Macmillan/Picador and BBC World.

She co-wrote the biography *My Life with Aids-Charmayne Broadway's Story* (Southern Books, South Africa 1998), and her children's fantasy *The Wise Enchanter* was published in 2006 by Bell Pond Books. She lives in Sarasota, Florida with her husband and son.

Printed in the United States
98590LV00005B/1-39/A